P9-BBN-324

THE MANAGER'S BIBLE

THE MANAGER'S BIBLE

How to Resolve 127 Classic Management Dilemmas

Carl Heyel

THE FREE PRESS
A Division of Macmillan Publishing Co., Inc.
NEW YORK

Collier Macmillan Publishers
LONDON

Copyright © 1981 by Clement Communications, Inc.

All rights reserved. No part of this book may be reproduced or
transmitted in any form or by any means, electronic or mechanical,
including photocopying, recording, or by any information storage
and retrieval system, without permission in writing from the
Publisher.

THE FREE PRESS
A Division of Macmillan Publishing Co., Inc.
866 Third Avenue, New York, N.Y. 10022

Collier Macmillan Canada, Ltd.

Library of Congress Catalog Card Number: 81-66434

Printed in the United States of America

printing number

1 2 3 4 5 6 7 8 9 10

Library of Congress Cataloging in Publication Data

Heyel, Carl
  The manager's bible

  Includes index.
  1. Management—Case studies.   I. Title.
HD31.H476   658   81-66434
ISBN 0-02-914680-1   AACR2

Contents

Part Two: DO

Part Three: CHECK

Part Four: THE PEOPLE EQUATION

A. Leadership and Motivation

B. Communicating

C. Start-Ups

Part Five: GET–AHEADS

Acknowledgment

Almost all of the scenarios herein appeared, sometimes in slightly altered form, in *Successful Supervision or The Better-Work Supervisor*, published by Clement Communications, Inc. (formerly Clemprint Incorporated), of Concordville, Pennsylvania. The author has been privileged to be associated with this publisher for many years, and is grateful for permission to incorporate here material he originally wrote for the publications mentioned.

THE MANAGER'S BIBLE

What this Book Is About

At our local Sunday school, a number of years ago, a distinguished visiting pastor from Scotland was addressing the lower grades in general assembly.

He held up a bright red apple, a McIntosh, and said he had a story to tell about apples and a little town in Scotland by the name of Applecross. This ancient town, he told us, actually began as a monastery founded in the year 673, one of the ancient centers of the Christian religion in Scotland. Among other things, the monastery was famous for the delicious apples grown by the monks. In fact, the whole surrounding country was famous for its apples, and the monks had to compete in the marketplace with all of the other apple growers.

The monks knew that their apples were as good as any of the others, and better than most, but they soon realized that what they needed was some distinguishing feature to mark their product. In this way, prospective purchasers would recognize them as the fruit of the monastery, and those who savored their taste wherever they may have purchased them would know where they had come from. So they hit upon a plan. Before the apples reddened in the sun, the monks went from tree to tree and painstakingly affixed on each of the yet-to-ripen fruit a small paper cross. Then when they gathered the ripened fruit they peeled off the paper, and there on each red apple was the "signature" of the monastery—a bright green cross where the sun had not colored the skin. That is how the village got its name, Applecross.

"And, my young friends," said our speaker, "that is what I want you to remember—the signature on the apples, the applecross. Just as the monks placed their imprint upon the fruit before it ripened, so your teachers here are trying to impress their imprint upon you while you are yet in the process of growing and developing. That will be their 'signature.' Do it honor."

Over the years I have often thought of the applecross story, and I sincerely trust that when all the accounts are in, the dedicated men and women who smoothed my own rough edges and beat some learning into my head will, wherever they are, see that I have brought no discredit upon their signatures.

Now why do I tell this story here—one that at first glance may seem far afield from the responsibilities of a manager? I do it to make a point. What if that Scottish pastor had told the youngsters to be good boys and girls, study hard, and mind their teachers? How long would his adjurations have stuck with them? And would I have remembered his little "sermon" with such vividness? Hardly.

And there's the point. *I remember the story,* and so I remember the message. And note also that even at their tender age, his listeners already knew the message the speaker was driving home. They all knew that they were supposed to do their homework and mind their teachers. But what the speaker did with his story—with his scenario, if you will, of the monastery and its apple orchard, and the monks with their little paper crosses—was to give his young listeners a new insight into the dedication of their teachers, the latter's desire to leave their mark upon them, and the students' responsibility to do honor to their efforts.

It works in every sort of communications situation. What if someone wanted to get across a point at a management seminar about the need for constant and unblinking vigilance against unnecessary costs and slack procedures? For an "applecross" scenario, he or she could hardly do better than to open with the following story abut the late J. Paul Getty, president of Getty Oil Company. Mr. Getty, who during his lifetime was often referred to as "the richest man in the world," had come up the hard way, knocking around oil fields, operating drill rigs, and always knowing his business inside out. And he always operated on the principle of keeping the overhead down. In his book, *How to Be Rich*, he tells the following story:

It seems that there were three executives in one of Mr. Getty's companies who irritated him no end. Every time he walked through their departments, he noticed all sorts of wasteful practices and signs of slipshod operations. He would always call these things to their attention, but nothing ever seemed to happen about them.

One day he instructed the company controller to withhold five dollars from each of the men's pay. When they inquired about it, the accounting department was to say that they were to see him, Getty, about the shortage.

Sure enough, Mr. Getty had three visitors on payday. He gave them each their five dollars, but also observed to each of them that it came as something of a surprise to him that they should have been so prompt to notice that five dollars came out of their own pockets, while they were letting hundreds of dollars slip away each week right in their own departments—dollars that ultimately came out of his, Mr. Getty's, pockets.

"Two of them got the point," Mr. Getty said. "They took the message to heart and mended their ways. The third did not—and not too long thereafter he was looking elsewhere for work."

Or suppose our seminar leader wanted to devote a session to employee attitudes and motivation. Here would be a ready-made scenario to drive home his basic point:

Jim Blake, supervisor, was relaxing at home, trying to read his newspaper. But he kept being interrupted by his small daughter. "Daddy," she'd say, "look at the new dress I put on my doll"—or "Daddy, come look at the new bonnet she's wearing!"

Finally, in desperation, he said, "Look, here's your sister's jigsaw puzzle. Let's see you put it together." He was sure that the puzzle would keep her busy for a good while—the picture to complete was a map of the world, with plenty of blue water that would make the pieces difficult to fit. But to Jim's surprise, after only a few minutes, the little girl was tugging at his arm to show him the completed map.

"How did you do it so fast?" he exclaimed.

"Well, you see," she explained, "there was a picture of a man on the other side. It was easy to put the man together in the box lid and flip the whole puzzle over. When the man was right, the whole world came out right too!"

"Fine—take it to Mother," said Jim, and added (to himself), "Brilliant kid—just like her old man!" But then it came to him—the moral for himself and his job in the little domestic episode: *When the individual man or woman is all right, the department and the company are all right, too!* Jim realized that if he and his fellow supervisors couldn't run their departments in such a way that the individual worker came out right, nothing that the higher-ups could do would ever make the "big picture" come out right.

A final example could be where the subject is the need for continuing awareness of the dependency of the "boss" on those who are working under him. The following scenario is quoted from Douglas McGregor's *The Human Side of Enterprise:*

> An agent of the Textile Workers Union of America likes to tell the story of the occasion when a new manager appeared in the mill where he was working. The manager came into the weave room the day he arrived. He walked directly over to the agent and said, "Are you Belloc?" The agent acknowledged that he was. The manager said, "I am the new manager here. When I manage a mill, I run it. Do you understand?" The agent nodded, and then waved his hand. The workers, intently watching this encounter, shut down every loom in the room immediately. The agent turned to the manager and said, "All right, go ahead and run it."

Now what do these three stories have in common? They all make their point by bringing to mind a vivid "moving picture" of a real-life episode. The reader (or listener) identifies with the story—lives it—and so remembers it. And, as stated earlier, by remembering the story, he or she remembers the message.

And speaking of messages, here is another interesting point about those scenarios. Consider them for a minute without reference to a particular seminar subject that you were told about ahead of time. If you let them stand alone, read them as is, and then reflect a bit on them, you will see that they are *multidimensional.* They all have a central thrust, but they provide varying insights, depending upon the angle from which you are looking at them, much as a diamond throws off different sparkles depending upon the light in which and the angle from which it is observed.

Thus, the Getty story, from one point of view, drives home a point about costs (Mr. Getty, the billionaire, being concerned about small details and little costs that add up to big overhead). But it is also a lesson on communication—the value of dramatizing a point in order to make it stick. And then again, it tells a lot about human nature—how people are always concerned about "Number One," about a few dollars when they come out of their own pockets rather than out of some impersonal company profit-and-loss statement.

Similarly, in the episode about Jim Blake and the jigsaw puzzle, we see immediately, of course, the point about the importance of the individual human being. But there's also a side-effect point in the structure of the story itself: how one can draw lessons from the most unexpected sources—in this case, literally out of the mouths of babes—and that it pays to keep our antennae out to make meaningful associations and "lateral thinking" connections.

Finally, Douglas McGregor's story, aside from its basic point of boss/employee dependency, triggers thinking on the general subject of the power of organized labor, on the general question of where loyalties lie in a work situation, and on individual arrogance and tactlessness.

All of which brings us to what this book is about, and how it goes about it. It's about managerial effectiveness and how to achieve it, and it goes about it by presenting a bookful of scenarios. The scenarios are real-life depictions—not, of course, recorded documentaries on real people and actual happenings in a strict reportorial sense, but brief dramatizations of situations that have actually happened, culled from ·many years of observation and direct experience. The Jim Blakes and other *dramatis personae* are all composites of actual supervisors and higher-level managers who found themselves in the situations described.

But specifically for whom have I presented these scenarios? What kind of reader do I envision? I have four kinds particularly in mind. In the first category is anyone who has a supervisory or middle-management position, and who aspires to rise higher on the management ladder. Such supervisors and managers will, I believe, find insights of value in these stories. The characters involved are representative of all types of industries, in all types of operations. I have striven to set forth their experiences, their solutions to problem situations and critical incidents, in a way that will enable anyone who reads about them to empathize with them—to step into their shoes and share the episodes from the inside.

What assumptions am I making about this type of reader? I am not envisioning someone who comes without any of the technical skills called for by his or her job, and who is looking for a basic "how to" text on specific techniques such as cost accounting, flexible budgeting, accounting controls, performance evaluation, and the like, although the scenarios do get into all of these subjects. Remember what I said in my opening story about the grade schoolers listening to the visitor from Scotland? They weren't being told anything they didn't basically know already; they were receiving reinforcement in something they knew. But beyond that, what they did know was being enriched and given new meaning, and was being fixed in their minds. Similarly, I feel that the insights provided by the scenarios will fortify anyone with a management position in the effective use of already quite widely known techniques. But note that many of the scenarios do expand upon the basic story line by including checklists or supplementary commentary for discussion and implementation. In this respect they go beyond the "applecross" narrative format.

Closely allied to this type of reader is a second type, namely the presupervisor and premanager, who is still in the ranks but aspires to make that first big step to supervisor or first-level department manager. The real-life scenarios should provide three-dimensional previews of the kinds of situations he or she will be up against once the coveted promotion has been achieved.

The third type of reader is the person who is involved in the conduct of supervisory training and management development programs. He or she will, I am sure, find it helpful to have at hand a ready source of "openers" that can serve as an effective launching pad from which to get off a discussion session on any managerial skill, be it in the area of planning, or operations and controls, or interpersonal relationships. I am assuming that he or she must always be on the lookout for effective ways of getting a message across, and I make bold to believe that this book will provide a welcome additional resource.

Finally, there is a fourth type of reader, welcomed to peer over the shoulders, so to speak, of the other three. These are higher-level executives whose own success rests upon the success of the first-line managers and supervisors reporting to them, and who will find the scenarios of help in providing inspiration and guidance to these subordinate executives.

A word about the order in which the scenarios are grouped and presented. Strictly speaking, if these little stories reflect real life, as I submit they do, I could simply have presented them in random fashion, in no particular order—for that is the way we are exposed to experience. The situations from which we learn do not present themselves in a nice procession of ordered learning steps, as would be the case with, say, a college curriculum. Rather, they come in haphazard sequence, usually in the form of emergency or crisis situations. As the years go by, and we have a chance to reflect upon our experiences, we categorize and organize them, so that by an intuitive information-retrieval process, the "seasoned" executive automatically and rapidly draws upon his memory bank and (depending upon the vividness of the experiences and the degree to which the lessons have been learned) makes the correct decision and takes the correct action, or at the very least, makes a better decision and takes a more effective action than he would have had he not had his experience to draw upon.

In order to shorten the categorization process and to facilitate information retrieval, I chose not to present my scenarios in haphazard sequence. Rather, I have ordered them under a broad set of headings. The headings are purposely broad, because to subdivide them too greatly (e.g., in encyclopedia format) would have been restrictive. It would be better, I felt, to group them as I have done, and to let the reader's imagination play over the stories to see in how many cases side-effect insights might make them applicable beyond their core message.

The groupings begin with the classic management formula of PLAN–DO–CHECK, and so the first three parts of this book embrace the operational aspects of the manager's job. With regard to these, by the time a manager is disposed to read a book like this, he or she will in varying measure have had some formal training. Even though they may know the techniques, however, the application of PLAN–DO–CHECK always becomes involved with people, for people are the medium through which the manager must work. Accordingly, following the first three parts, a large fourth part is added, under the heading of THE PEOPLE EQUATION. This is further broken down into eight subdivisions: *leadership and motivation; communicating; start-ups; training; rules and regulations; critical incidents; exits;* and *the customer's-eye view.* Finally, Part Five, GET–AHEADS, focuses on situations dealing with the supervisor's and manager's personal advancement.

That finishes the prologue. Now let's get on with the show. . .

PART ONE

PLAN

Fred Writes a Speech

"Homework tonight?" asked Fred Able's wife, as she watched him elaborately sharpen some pencils, shift the lamp on her just-cleared dining-room table, and sit down with a pad of paper in front of him and a dictionary within reach.

"I've got to get started on my speech," he replied, somewhat self-importantly. "They tapped me to talk at that supervisors' 'retreat' we're having next month."

"What's the subject?" she inquired. "TV Spectator Sports, I hope—you're an expert on that!"

"No wisecracks, please," said Fred. "I'm talking on 'The Supervisor and Contingency Planning.' I've been stewing it around in the back of my mind for days now, but I haven't hit on a good angle as yet. There will be some v.p.s there, and I've gotta make a good showing."

"Pooh," said his wife. "Any housewife could write that speech. Contingencies are our way of life. Why just the other day—"

"Yeah, honey, I know," said Fred, amused but only listening with half an ear. ("These women," he thought indulgently, "they should spend a day at the shop. They think they have a big crisis when the baby spills milk on the carpet!") He began to concentrate on writing his speech, with his wife's voice chattering away in the background. But then he began taking in what she was saying.

"—and remember when Lucille and Harry and their kids and Lucille's mother came in on us unexpectedly that Sunday? And I had to dream up a dinner for seven grownups and seven kids, when all I had been planning on was hamburgers and leftovers? It's a good thing I keep a special set of canned goods and ready-mix desserts for just such emergencies. You yourself talked about that spiced ham for weeks—"

1. Check inventory of spares and critical supplies, Fred wrote on his pad of paper. *Never, so to speak, "let your cupboard be bare."*

"You're so right, honey," he murmured.

"—and remember when I had to be in the hospital for three weeks for that operation?" his wife went on. "You'll also remember that I worked with Joey for three weeks ahead of that, so he could prepare some simple meals, and take care of things while Sis went off to that Girl Scout jamboree. You were well taken care of, as I recall."

"Yes," Fred replied, "both kids turned out to be real cooks." And he wrote on his pad: *2. Cross-train employees to fill in on emergencies.*

"—and with prices what they are," said his wife, "every housewife has to learn to make do with what she has, no matter what. For example, the way the kids grow, it's a caution, the clothes they need. When Clarabelle was invited to that party, I fixed her up with a dress out of two old ones of Sue's, and she was the belle of the ball, if I do say so myself."

"That's my girl," said Fred approvingly, as he wrote on his pad: *3. Encourage innovation and initiative. Arrange equipment and facilities for maximum flexibility in sudden redeployment demands.*

"—and last winter's ten-day power failure was no joke," continued Fred's Mrs. "But it would have been a lot worse if I hadn't been prepared with those emergency coal-oil lamps and that supply of Sterno for Joey's cook-out equipment. We had hot soup and coffee every day, four-minute eggs for breakfast, and TV dinners at night (without the TV, of course)."

"They didn't eat that well at the hotel downtown," agreed Fred, and wrote: *4. Evaluate stand-by facilities, and check periodically to be sure all such units are in working order.*

"Of course, there was pretty much of a mess to clean up when the power came back on, what with coal-oil soot and broken lamp chimneys and Sterno stains and all those fireplace ashes. Lucky the housewives in the neighborhood pool their list of women available for daywork, or I'd have had a breakdown. Goodness knows I don't need a maid, but a woman every now and then sure helps—"

"You managed beautifully, dear," said Fred, and wrote: 5. *Have a continuing arrangement with a reliable temporary help contractor, for emergency fill-in personnel.*

"—of course, now that Susan's in the eighth grade, things are a bit easier. She's a real helper, that kid. Can do practically everything now that I do."

"Great kid," murmured Fred, and wrote down: *6. Develop reliable understudy.*

"My goodness," said his wife, suddenly conscience stricken. "Here I've been chattering away and keeping you from working on your speech. I'm terribly sorry, Fred."

"Oh, that's all right, honey," said Fred magnanimously, as he pocketed his notes and put away pencils and paper. "Always glad to hear about your problems and make suggestions when I can. . . . . And," he added, reaching for the *TV Guide*, "I did manage to jot down a few ideas for my speech."

"What If I Don't Pull It Off?"

George Goodman had recently been promoted from the job of supervisor of an important department to department head with a number of supervisors reporting to him. And then his troubles began.

George had been a good operating man who worked well with his people and got the work out on time with only rare quality problems. Management had tagged him as a "bright young man" to watch and to push ahead. He was proud that he had been selected for the new job, especially since he had been jumped over some senior men whose experience was considerably longer than his. He was determined to live up to management's expectations for him, no matter how difficult that might be. In truth, he was pretty awed by the size of his new responsibilities. "What if I don't pull it off?" he kept asking himself.

In his desire not to make any mistakes, George soon found himself keeping a constant personal check on practically every phase of his operations. He organized an elaborate system of reporting for his supervisors, so that he could keep absolutely up to date on an enormous number of details.

Result: A flood of reports, questions, and messages came to his desk every day. His working day grew alarmingly long. His constant complaint was that "there just wasn't enough time" in the average working day to get his job done—as *he* felt it had to be done. He stayed in his office late. He took work home. He became irritable and short-tempered with his family.

One day the vice president of operations, on a visit from the home office, "just happened" to drop in for a chat with George. (He

14

was the one who had recommended him for the new job.) George was as usual buried in paperwork, but he shoved everything aside to talk to the boss. They talked about how things were going, and the v.p. raised some questions about a recent small snafu in one of George's departments.

George was immediately on the defensive and got into a rather heated lament about how things had piled up, how the pressure was mounting, repeating that there "just wasn't enough time" in the normal working day (which had almost regularly become a twelve-hour day in his case).

The vice president heard him out, interjecting suitably sympathetic sounds, and George was congratulating himself that at last he was getting the home office to see how tough things actually were at his end when the boss suddenly pulled a piece of paper out of his pocket.

"Look, George," he said, "I've got to run along. I've been looking forward to having a talk with you. I've been keeping an eye on your operation, and I know you've been having some problems. That's why I'm giving you this," and he handed the paper to George. "I'm convinced that your problem isn't in your ability to run your job, but rather in the fact that you've been letting the job run you. What you have to do is invest some time in organizing and planning for *exception management*, so that you can do what we're paying you to do—namely, *planning* and *controlling*, rather than putting out fires."

"Exception management?" said George, puzzled, as he began unfolding the paper.

"Never mind the details now," said the v.p., getting up and heading for the door. "What I've given you is simply a guideline on basics—questions that cover the president's job, my job, and I'm sure *your* job. Look upon them as homework you have to do about your job. I'm not looking for formal answers to the 'quiz questions.' Just think about 'em and put 'em to work!" And he left.

The v.p. was right in saying that the questions he gave George apply to any job. They're listed below:

The Vice President's List for Exception Management

1. What are the principal types of decisions that must be made by you for your department?

2. Which of these call for true judgmental analysis each time, and which can be codified into *choices* among predetermined alternatives?
3. Do you have a manual in the department to cover standard operating procedures? Do individual supervisors and operators (where appropriate) have pertinent manual sections?
4. When was the last audit made to see whether standard operating procedure manuals are up to date? Is there an established procedure and fixed responsibility for *keeping* them up to date?
5. How many crisis situations was your department up against during the past year? Were these similar enough to previous situations that a standard operating procedure could have prevented any or all of them or greatly speeded their resolution?
6. Have checkpoints been established at which "readings" are taken and predetermined lines of action followed?
7. Is input information that comes to you so organized as to concentrate only on exception situations?
8. In the light of all of the above, have ranges of responsibility and action been established for subordinates, for automatic handling by them, with parameters for exception situations that must be brought to you?

What Would Happen to Your Department If You Weren't There?

Let's consider a story about Mr. X, the chief executive of a large corporation.

Mr. X stopped off at the office of his eye doctor one morning, because of a slight but troublesome fault in vision he had been experiencing. There were times when he could see only half of each letter on a page he was reading—like the effects of a sudden glare.

After thorough tests and examination, the specialist faced him soberly. "I'll have to give it to you straight, Frank," he said. "The right eye is in trouble—rather serious trouble. I'm afraid you're in for some extended treatment."

The executive blinked a little and began thinking of his crowded schedule and how he'd be able to fit in a series of visits. "Well, I'll work it in somehow," he said. "When do we start?"

"As a matter of fact," the specialist said, "this is going to call for a hospital stay."

"Hospital!" exclaimed Mr. X. "Now you're hitting my schedule where it really hurts. What's the score? Is it as serious as all that?"

"I'll put the cards on the table," replied the doctor. "You're suffering from retracting retinas. I know we can save the left eye, but the other one is not too good. This will require at least three months in a hospital. Complete rest. No head motions. No reading. No television. For a while, no visitors, no phones."

17

Mr. X gave a low whistle, and leaned back to absorb this news. He knew he was talking to a top man in his field. A second opinion wouldn't change the verdict. Finally he said, "Well, if it's got to be, it's got to be. I'll be in touch with you. There's a lot I've got to do in the next few weeks to handle this thing. What'll happen to XYZ Company, God only knows."

"Frank," said the doctor gently, "just take a deep breath and listen to me. This isn't any 'don't call me, I'll call you' affair. You're going to the hospital this afternoon."

"This afternoon?" This was a real body blow for Mr. X! He looked at the doctor in disbelief. "It can't be done," he said, shaking his head.

"It's as simple as this," said the doctor briskly. "Do you want to save that one eye—and I hope both—or do you want to be blind because of some hassle at XYZ? I'm going to call the hospital, and you're going to call Mrs. X, and then we'll carry on from there."

The upshot was that Mr. X went to the hospital immediately. The world didn't come to an end. His staff closed ranks. The momentum of projects he had started was ample to carry them on.

While absolute quiet and no reading were imposed for an extended period, there were no doctor's orders against *thinking*, and Mr. X did a lot of that. The thought of what would have been his personal problem had the light really gone out was a sobering one, and put his whole job in new a perspective.

Luckily for him he had the kind of staff competence and staff loyalty that kept things together. But he saw clearly that neither he nor any of his department heads could afford to leave such an important matter to chance. He resolved to see to it that there was some real planning in all departments on that one.

Security Planning

"What are you doing with the Zilch Company's computer manual?" asked the factory manager as he peered over his assistant's shoulder at the book he held open in front of him. George Carter, newly appointed to the assistant job after several years as a supervisor, had obviously been taking copious notes, as a sheaf of closely written ruled pages testified. "You've come up with some pretty good ideas since you've been on this job," the boss added, "but I hope you haven't made a deal with IBM to install a computer out there."

"No," said George, "but there are some darn good ideas for us in this computer manual, and not limited to a computer, either. I borrowed it from my brother-in-law. He's a programmer over at Zilch's."

"So how do we stand to gain from a computerless computer manual?" the factory manager wanted to know.

"Well, you know all the fuss that's been made about *security*—facilities and information—now that that whole NASA project is being moved down here, and we're giving that annex over to the R&D boys on the development contract," George explained. "Joe—my brother-in-law—was telling me about all the furor that's been developing recently about computer security. You've seen those news stories about sabotage and theft—especially the leakage of confidential information from computer operations.

"When Joe showed me this computer security manual, I immediately saw that it was full of ideas that applied directly to our situation, and so I borrowed it. You've been talking a lot about

19

contingency planning recently. Well, here are some pointers about *preventive* planning—handling contingencies by not letting them happen in the first place."

George showed some of his pages of notes to the factory manager. "Look," he said, "I've copied out the parts that make just as much sense for our NASA project as they do for any computer installation."

Here are George's notes:

1. With respect to *theft of property, access to premises,* and *prevention of physical disaster:* See to it that all responsible line managements double-check on all of the normal protective, preventive, surveillance, and housekeeping facilities:
   - More guards?
   - More stringent rules about passes?
   - A new look at fire prevention measures?
   - A reexamination of the fire-fighting setup?
   - Provisions for standby power?
   - Adequate all-night lighting?
   - A new look at entrances and exits, locks, electric surveillance (à la the airlines) for detection of firearms and other weapons?
2. Re *records:*
   - Is there a procedure for designating which files, programs, and related documentation require duplication and *separate storage?*
   - Have legal requirements for file retention been investigated?
   - Should the location of the sensitive operation staff be reconsidered, re environmental hazards (e.g., near airport, structural inadequacies of present buildings, etc.)?
3. Re *information vulnerability:*
   - Are common-sense precautions taken—such as shredders for destruction of records to be discarded, strict rules on handling extra carbons by users?
   - Are all reports issued by the sensitive operation necessary?
   - Is the list of who gets reports checked periodically?
   - Have collusion opportunities for theft of proprietary information been checked?

- Are there adequate identification and authorization codes for requests for information made from remote points by phone, wire, or computer terminals?
- Should scramblers be used on certain communication lines?
- Is an escort provided for all visitors?

4. Re *personnel:*

- One disloyal or disgruntled employee is ten times as dangerous as any external security threat. Therefore, complete security means careful selection, checking, training, and motivation of all personnel in sensitive areas. If these factors are neglected, putting a sensitive operation inside Fort Knox won't suffice!

Uptight about Downtime

The plant manager had called his supervisors together for the weekly planning session. "In general," he said, "you fellows are doing a good job of production planning and scheduling—especially considering our big volume increase over the past year.

"I appreciate your problems of breaking in additional help, stretching our equipment capacities to the limit, and having operators get the hang of some of our new machines. But even so, I think you're experiencing too many interruptions to planned production because of machine failures, or machine malfunctions that cause you to do work over and to lose time while repairs and adjustments are made.

"So today we're going to cut short the discussion of immediate schedules, unless one of you has a real emergency situation, and concentrate on the general problem of *preventive maintenance*. Let's kick around all possible ideas you have to lick this problem of machine downtime without having to spend a million dollars— which we haven't got!—for a brand new plant and brand new equipment."

A lively discussion ensued, because everyone had some ideas on the subject. Here's what it all boiled down to in terms of guidelines for all supervisors to follow in the future:

A special coaching program for all of the newer people in every department was to be inaugurated, concentrating specifically on preventive maintenance, proper loading of machines, proper speeds, special sounds and other danger signals to listen and look for that warn about something not just right in the way equipment is operating, specific cleaning and lubricating responsibilities of the operator, and so on. For every employee less than six months in a department, an experienced man was to be assigned as "coach," to keep a special eye on the handling of tools and machines, answer any questions, and render required assistance where the new employee was experiencing difficulties.

A "PMP" list was to be prepared for each major piece of equipment—"PMP" standing for "Preventive Maintenance Pointers"—and posted prominently at each machine location. This would include points on the prescribed way to start up the machine, what to do for possible types of jam-ups, information on speeds and feeds, the kind of danger signals mentioned above, cleaning and lubricating pointers, and the like.

The maintenance foreman was to check with all operating supervisors, and come up with a "Weak Sisters" list of equipment—i.e., the relatively few machines that were causing the most trouble. He would report back to the plant manager on these, especially with respect to the following points:

- The adequacy of spare parts in stores, based on the availability of parts from the machine supplier and other sources.
- Any machines for which special plans should be made to take them out of service temporarily for overhaul.
- Hazards to safety that might exist, with suggestions for eliminating or reducing.
- Machine or machines recommended for earliest replacement possible.

On certain of the new equipment, the plant manager arranged with the supervisors involved to schedule an after-hours meeting (employees would be paid for the time) at which a representative of the manufacturer would be present to give special information and instructions on operation and proper upkeep.

"OK, fellows," the plant manager summed up, "I think you've come up with a solid program. Let's schedule another one of these 'state-of-the-nation' sessions four weeks from now, to compare notes on progress."

Full-Time Solutions with Part-Time Employees

"We'll just have to go into another shift, or at least work some kind of part-time shift arrangement, Joe," the plant superintendent said to Joe Decker, production supervisor. "I know the scheduling problem is going to be tough, but—"

"I've been thinking about that," said Joe. "And I think the answer is to establish a regular program of hiring part-time workers. For this extra shift, they could *all* be part-timers—and I could easily make special arrangements for supervision."

"But wouldn't you have more headaches than the program would be worth?" the boss wanted to know. "Maybe part-time workers are only part-*interested* workers, and probably with little or no experience."

"Not from what I hear," countered Joe. "But let me look into it a little more and report back."

So Joe did some inquiring, supplemented by some intensive research in the business-press file of the local library. Here is what he found:

Many companies have been hiring part-timers to solve scheduling problems. However, more and more companies that started out with a simple scheduling problem like Joe's are discovering that part-timers provide other benefits as well. A recent Labor Department study found that part-time employees generally provide higher productivity, greater loyalty, and less absenteeism than full-time employees, while putting less strain on company payrolls. The

24

study, covering sixty-eight major corporations, concluded: "Employers are going to be money ahead using part-timers."

Recruitment apparently presents no problem. Part-time work is preferred by many people for a variety of reasons. Younger, female, older, and handicapped workers especially are seeking such jobs because of family responsibilities, health problems, or mere personal choice. As a result, a new kind of classification has come into being: "permanent part-time" workers.

Incidentally, many manufacturing and light-assembly plants in suburban areas offer "mothers' hours," roughly from 9 A.M. to 2:30 P.M., to attract local women with school-age children.

NOTE: Joe noted, in a Wall Street Journal *rundown on the subject, that Giant Food Inc., a Washington-based retailer, reported sampling the tardiness records of 12,000 employees, 5,000 of whom work part-time. The average full-timer's rate of late arrivals cost the company 7.4 days of work a year, twice the rate of time lost because of the average part-timer's tardiness.*

Topsy-Turvy Priorities

Rosemary Anderson was the office supervisor for a large legal firm. For some time she had been hoping to have the firm invest in one of those new, automated typewriter installations, complete with a "minicomputer" electronic brain that stored keyed-in information for later recall, automatically took care of spacing, permitted correction of errors by simple overtyping, permitted insertion of special paragraphs into form letters, and all the rest. It handled corrections on manuscripts (stored in memory until ready to run), and automatically renumbered pages as required. Once set, it could run any number of perfect copies.

So Rosemary did a lot of pencil work and presented the head of the firm with detailed figures on how the efficiency of the typists and secretaries would be stepped up with the new automated equipment, how they wouldn't have to fuss with corrections and retypings and messy carbons, how good secretaries were hard to get and hard to keep, and all the rest.

But to her disappointment, the answer was a definite "No!" There wasn't enough leeway in the budget, business being what it was; her people would just have to do with their existing equipment, messy carbons and all.

However, after doing some more thinking about the matter, Rosemary decided not to take no for an answer. So she completely redid her pencil work, and came back with an entirely new approach.

"Look," she said, "We've completely missed the point about the real productivity and profit potential that we can get with this new

26

word-processing setup. In fact, it would be cheap at twice the price!

"Consider what happened in our conference room just yesterday afternoon: six high-priced lawyers—three of our own, two representing XYZ Company, and one government man—had to sit around the table, waiting to review the next draft being typed of that complicated merger deal. Every time a new phase of the agreement was worked out, that scenario was repeated. And incidentally, in the rush crisis atmosphere, some of those pages were full of typos and smudgy erasure.

"But here's the main point I'm making—*we've clearly got our priorities topsy-turvy if we're worrying about whether the equipment investment is worth saving a nickel a page on typing costs, while the meter is ticking away on those lawyers at the rate of $300 an hour!*"

Rosemary got her machine.

A President Asks a "Simple" Question

One day the president of a large corporation asked his vice president of Marketing how the sales managers of the various districts made decisions about which potential buyers the salesmen contacted. The president reasoned that the total sales force was just too small to see all of the possible users of the company's products. "I'm just curious," he told the Marketing v.p., "as to how the decisions are made for allocating sales-force time."

The vice president referred the question to the sales manager, who passed it along to the district managers. The report came back that the individual sales representatives made the decisions about which potential buyers to visit.

This led to a lot of other questions, such as: how did the sales representatives make these decisions? What information about the sales potential of each customer in a territory was given to a sales representative? What kind of scores were communicated between districts, showing average sales per call and percentage of potential sales represented by the sales actually made?

Thus a simple question asked by the president led to the discovery that sales representatives, who were given very little guidance from management, were making the critical decisions on how over $25 million in sales-force expenditures were used. This discovery resulted in a decision to do an analysis of how the sales representatives allocated their time. This in turn led to the discovery that many high-potential customers were not seen at all,

28

and many relatively low-potential customers were seen too frequently. Now statistical analyses of territorial potentials versus performance are used to establish scientifically based call schedules and salesmen itineraries, and computerized reports have been instituted to show comparative sales and sales-to-potential ratios by territories.

Moral for managers: Look for simple questions—they often lead to big answers.

Al Goodmark Hangs on to His Good People

Al Goodmark and the plant's personnel director were having an uncomfortable discussion. Uncomfortable, because they were confronted with a problem that looked as though it was going to result in bad news for nine valued employees.

The company was in the business of manufacturing components for data-processing equipment and had been experiencing a protracted slack in orders as their manufacturing-company customers were adjusting to severe industry dislocations.

"It looks as though we're just going to have to let those nine people in your A and B departments go, Al," said Frank Evans, the personnel director. "You've been carrying them on essentially 'make-work' projects, and you know that that can't go on forever."

"I know," replied Al, "what I've got them on will last only for the rest of this week. But I don't want to say anything to them yet. I want to see if Special Contracts can possibly close one of those pending deals in time to do my gang any good—although frankly I doubt it. But don't push me for a few days yet. I just know that a week after I lose those people we'll suddenly be swamped with work, and I'll be up against it."

"Okay," said Frank, "but remember that all you're doing now is gambling."

Al said he wanted to sleep on the problem, but he didn't really mean that. He wanted some more time to *think* about the problem. And he did. He came back with a real zinger of an idea. Frank saw

30

the possibilities immediately, and together they worked on it with results that were even better than they had hoped for. Here's what they did:

They decided to go into the "temporary help" business. Using their combined contacts, they talked to and wrote to electronic companies in a wide radius of their plant, to see if they would like to take on some experienced personnel for specific periods—preferably ninety days. The nine workers would remain on their home company's payroll, and would retain their home-base seniority. The home company would pay all fringe benefits, and simply bill the using companies for their time, at their regular rates.

The proposition found takers almost immediately. "As a matter of fact," Frank Evans reported later, "I didn't have to go beyond the letter B in the electronics manufacturers directory."

As a result of Al's idea, not only was the company able to hang on to some good people, but there was an added bonus in the form of boosted company morale throughout the plant.

Snafu: A Lesson from History

On Saturday morning, February 20, 1971, at 9:33, a human error put Americans on a false-alarm emergency alert that was to be used in a nuclear attack. Before the furor died down, the nation had a dramatic public demonstration of the kind of holes that can be moth-eaten into even the most vital, well-thought-out contingency plan by neglect, human fallibility, lack of proper practice trials, purposeful disregard of established procedure, and sheer dunderheadedness.

It was forty minutes before the error was cleared up at the National Emergency Warning Center at Cheyenne Mountain, Colorado.

As pieced together later: An employee at the center, in a mixup of punched tapes prepared in advance, put a message on the wire to the country's radio and television stations saying that the president had declared a national emergency, and that all normal broadcasting was to cease "immediately." The message carried the code word "hatefulness," which was to be used only in the event of a real alert.

In the not-so-funny comedy of errors that followed, a number of stations around the country did go off the air after advising listeners and viewers of the "emergency." Others, instead of following procedure immediately, checked and determined that the transmission was a mistake, and continued normal broadcasting—which turned out well in the light of subsequent events but was a breach of procedure nevertheless.

The National Emergency Warning Center frantically tried to

cancel the message, but the trouble was that in accordance with standard contingency procedure, a certain code word was required to cancel the message, just as the correct code word "hatefulness" was required to authenticate it in the first place. And the nerve center of our defense information system couldn't find the cancellation code word, "impish," to confirm that the cancellation was authentic. The false alert looked exactly like the real one. Therefore, the fact that many broadcasting stations blandly took it upon themselves not to follow the procedure called for has raised serious questions about the effectiveness of our vaunted civilian warning system.

The warning center is part of the nuclear alert complex in the base of Cheyenne Mountain, ten miles south of Colorado Springs. Protected by thick concrete, it is operated by the Office of Civil Defense. The communications operations are staffed by civilian employees of the Army Strategic Communications Command.

In a real nuclear alert, warning of impending attack would come from North American Air Defense Command (NORAD) in the mountain, which operates radar warning systems ringing the United States and Canada. The warning should then be transmitted to the American and Canadian Joint Chiefs of Staff, to the U.S. and Canadian governments, to the Polaris missile fleet, Strategic Air Command, and to the National Emergency Warning Center. The latter is the link to the civilian population.

The warning center is directly connected into the Associated Press and United Press International radio news wires, and these in turn go to the country's broadcasting stations. The circuit is supposedly tested at least twice a week, and there is an elaborate system of codes which is supposed to make the kind of snafu that occurred impossible.

Every three months, each radio and TV station is sent a list of code words for each day. These *must* be included in a message if an actual alert is in progress. There are also special code words for use in unscheduled tests. For authentic messages there are two code words—one for a message announcing an alert, and one for a message ending the alert. For February 20, 1971, as stated earlier, these two words were, respectively, "hatefulness" and "impish." Two tests of the wire are scheduled each week: 9:30 A.M. Saturday and 8:30 P.M. Sunday. They are preceded by the words "Testing Emergency Action Notification System." To keep the stations (supposedly) on their toes, unscheduled test messages, using special code words, are also sent. Messages for both tests and the real thing are prepared in advance on punched paper tapes that reproduce messages on teletype machines.

What happened on February 20 was that an operator sent the tape prepared for a real alert instead of the tape for a test.

On receipt of a real alert, stations are supposed to announce immediately that the president has directed an "emergency action notification," and then go off the air—unless they happen to be "key" stations. These stations are supposed to keep broadcasting news bulletins, emergency instructions, and the like.

In view of all of the above precautions, what happened after the false alert is almost unbelievable. Many stations just didn't know the procedure. Others, instead of doing what they should have done, listened to see if their competitors had gone off the air. Some took it upon themselves to use their own means of checking the authenticity of the alert. Some, because they knew a test had been scheduled for 9:30, simply ignored the warning! The Office of Civil Defense has stated that it has no estimate of how many of the nation's 5,000 radio and 800 television stations responded properly to the alert.

Indicative of the extent of the snafu: Soon after the false alert was sent out, the National Warning Center realized the error. A message was sent saying "This is the National Warning Center—Cancel EAN (Emergency Action Notification) tape sent at 9:33 EST." But, since "hatefulness" was the code to *initiate* an alert, not to *end* it, stations should properly have ignored that message, too. At 10:13, the center at long last found the right formula: "Message authenticator: Impish/Impish—Cancel message sent at 9:33 EST."

The crisis was over.

Contingency planning performance appraisal: *negative, in spades.*

Can You Sing Something Simple?

A large company drew up plans for a spectacular new die-casting plant to make parts for its new outboard motor. Management wanted the finest fully automated die-casting plant in the country. The chief industrial engineer was given the job of touring the country to find the ultimate in automation. When he came back, he said that full automation was indeed workable, but that the knottiest problem was devising an automatic conveyor system for carting off metal scrap from the die-casting machines.

Studies then showed that it would be possible to automate the scrap handling, but that it would require an investment of $180,000. However, there was a happy ending. The final solution to the scrap disposal problem: one man with a wheelbarrow.

Ma Bell's Executive Time Trimmer

It was going to take George Foster two and a half hours to fight his way through king-sized traffic tie-ups from company headquarters in mid-Manhattan back to the New Jersey town where the company had its main plant, and where George lived. He was good and mad, because he had promised to take his wife out to dinner, and he would now be lucky if he got home before eight o'clock.

"I'm really going to do something about the waste of time in getting back and forth whenever we have these merchandising-production planning meetings in New York," he fumed. Ed Byer, the plant purchasing man, who always made the trek with him and had half-dozed off, grunted agreement. "Like what?" he asked, rousing himself.

"Look," said George, "how long have you and I been going to these meetings with our records and projections on production schedules and bottle and jar purchases, and the latest cost dope on new package designs and package samples, to work with Sales on the new product lines and design changes and shipping deadlines and all the rest?" (The company was in the cosmetics business, with high-prestige items and fancy packaging, highly seasonal style changes, and all the other complexities that demanded frequent get-togethers between Production Planning and Purchasing and Plant Operations on the one hand, and the heads of Sales and Merchandising and Advertising on the other. With sales headquarters in New York City, where all the buyers came, and the plant in

Jersey, this meant treks back and forth—three or four people from the plant slogging over to New York, and alternately a lot of high-priced selling, advertising, and merchandising people beating their way to the factory.)

"You and I have been doing this for six years at least, and Fred Burke for longer than that," said Ed.

"Exactly," George agreed. "And Al Keene's been v.p. for Sales for ten years, and the head of Advertising and Packaging for almost that long."

"What's that got to do with anything, and especially with this traffic?" Ed wanted to know.

"Just this," replied George. "We've all been working together for a long time. We know each others' voices and inflections and mannerisms. We could understand each other perfectly if we were in separate rooms, we at the plant hearing what the New York gang is saying, and they hearing us, without being able to see each other."

"So?" said Ed.

"What I'm getting at," said George, "is that it's ridiculous for us to waste all this time traveling back and forth. I've been talking to our Bell Systems representative, and with the instruments as they've developed them today, we can do all the meeting we need over a conference hookup. We'll spread all our papers on the table in the plant conference room, and Al Keene and his gang can do the same with their records and projections in New York. With the telephone hookups now available, we can talk back and forth without anybody's having to manipulate buttons or saying 'Over and out,' or 'Roger,' or any of that jazz. And as I say, since we all know each other's voices, nobody has to introduce himself before talking. It's a cinch!"

"But what about the samples and sketches?" asked Ed.

"We'll send 'em over by messenger before the meeting," George explained. "And for refinement, we can think about facsimile. No problem."

"Sounds okay to me," said Ed. "Let's get the boss to do something about it."

And they did. And it worked like a charm.

NOTE: What George was talking about was the Bell System's Speakerphone configuration. Operated in conjunction with a regular telephone, the arrangement consists of two units—a control pad and a loudspeaker—each of which may be placed wherever the user desires. The control pad contains the ON/QUIET and OFF buttons, the volume adjustment control, and the microphone. The loudspeaker unit houses the electrical circuitry used in the system, in addition to the loudspeaker itself.

An important feature is the omnidirectional microphone. All members of a small group sitting around a table can be heard equally well, because the microphone picks up sound directed at it from all angles. The set has voice-controlled switching. The caller's voice turns on the switching mechanism, and his voice (or the entire group's) is transmitted to the other caller.

Only one party or group can speak at one time. If both parties try to talk simultaneously, the person speaking the loudest will transmit. This feature caused some interesting shouting matches at first, with Al Keene's and George Foster's free-wheeling groups trying to "get the floor." But they soon developed a smoothly working discipline. They still argue, loud and clear, but they argue one at a time.

A parting thought on planning

In making plans, managers must often treat as fixed, things which are essentially variable. But they must also be ready to change as evidence of this variability advances upon them. Those who can't change their *minds*, can't change anything else.

—*Henry M. Boettinger*

PART TWO

DO

"When He's Standing Idle, He's Worth $$$ to Me!!"

**The Case of the Foreman Who Knew
What He Was Talking About**

Charlie Pearson was a foreman in an electronics plant. His department consisted of five lines of automatic machines called "rollers," which produce small capacitors at high speed from rolls of insulating material and interleaving foil. Five women on each line each handled five machines simultaneously, moving from machine to machine, inserting rolls as required, and keeping an eye on indicator dials counting output.

Backing up the women were three roll-machine adjusters (recently increased from two) for the whole department—skilled mechanics who took care of basic setups, made refined adjustments, and got the machines started again if a tear in the material caused a stoppage.

As often happens in the best of plants, a sharp austerity program was in full swing, as management tried to cut costs to the bone to meet a tough competitive situation. As part of this drive, a firm of industrial consultants had been called in, and every operation was being fine-combed for possible savings. The consultants did a forced-draft job of time study, "tally-sheet studies" showing checks of departmental manning against output, "ratio-delay" studies, and the like. By certain method changes, improvement in scheduling, and a general tightening up of operations, they were able to make some impressive showings.

43

When they got to Charlie's department, they immediately targeted in on the adjusters. "Our tally-sheet and ratio-delay analyses show that the man-equivalent of one-and-a-half adjusters is standing idle at all times in the roll machine department," they reported to management. "Obviously, one man can be eliminated. We recommend this work-force reduction immediately. Projected saving: $19,500 per year."

The plant manager called Charlie in and said, "How come you were able to sweet-talk me into that extra man? Here are the facts and figures. We're going to have to cut you back to two adjusters."

But Charlie had done some tally sheeting of his own, long before the engineers had arrived on the scene. Before requesting the additional adjuster, he had kept a careful record of output per hour per machine on each line, for every day for three consecutive weeks, noting downtime and reasons therefor. He had kept similar detailed records after management had authorized the new man, to confirm what he suspected would be the case.

The outcome was even more dramatic than he had expected: That extra adjuster manpower was just what he needed to keep his lines running, with the workers moving rhythmically from machine to machine, and with roll breakage either anticipated and prevented, or taken care of promptly. Charlie had meant to wait another week to make his findings airtight, but with the boss's edict, he brought his tallies to the front office, where a meeting with the engineers had been set up.

"Spoilage and idle time under the two-adjuster arrangement amounted to several times the cost of the extra man, not counting customer complaints and bollixing up shipments," he pointed out. "You engineers have the wrong slant on this situation. *The more those adjusters are idle, the better off my department is.* It means that all machines are running smoothly and five women on a line are turning out productive work!"

Draconian Measures

Draco was a tough-minded ancient Greek lawmaker. He set death as the penalty for most infractions, and legend has it that his laws were written in blood. Hence today the term, "Draconian measures," refers to the sternest possible last-ditch lines of action laid down to save an almost hopeless situation.

When competition really gets tough, management may have to take Draconian measures simply to stay in business. Here are two examples from real life:

A hundred-year-old drug and pharmaceutical company, with sales in the $250 million range, had a fall-off in profits of almost 33 percent over a seven-year period. This was in the face of a 77 percent rise in the industry's profits over the same period.

A leading figure in the drug industry was brought in to save the situation. He immediately overhauled management, revitalized research and development, and launched a hard-hitting, cost-cutting program.

His cost cutting went into the most remote corners of operations. For example, the company was using about a million eggs a week in which to grow vaccines. The labs were throwing the unused portions of the eggs away. He saw to it that the company sold the yolks to mink breeders, and also looked into the possibility of selling the shells as a source of lime for plant food. "Nobody around here ever seemed to worry about avoidable waste," the new president told a *Business Week* interviewer. A number of executives were asked to leave, along with rank-and file-personnel reduction. "This is a business organization," he told the reporter, *"and the individual has to learn about the profit motive."*

45

   The other example has to do with a tough-minded new management that took over the running of an aircraft-parts manufacturing company that had fallen upon bad times. The firm was losing more than $100,000 a month. At first the losses were merely in one division, but soon other divisions ran into trouble as their managers were moved into the "sick" division to bolster operations.

   The new president decided to divide the company into four operating divisions and invited the managers, including department heads, to his home. They were asked to put the name of every employee—about eight hundred, at that time—on separate pieces of paper. The president then told the managers to pick up the names of the people they *really* needed to operate their divisions. When all were satisfied, *there were more than three hundred names still on the table!*

Is Your Company Paying for "Mustard on the Plate"?

"Our profits," remarked the head of a large importer and processor of mustard and other spices, "come largely from the mustard *left on the plate.*" He was referring to the well-known phenomenon that the diner at home as well as in the restaurant will heap mustard on the side of his plate, and then use only a bit of it, leaving the rest of it to be poured down the drain by the dishwasher.

That may be a profit for the seller of mustard, but the habit represents a pure loss to anyone who conforms to that pattern.

How much is your company losing in every department, because of "mustard left on the plate"—supplies carelessly used and wasted, material spoiled through poor workmanship (along with the labor that went into it and the overhead it was supposed to support), a future sale lost because of a discourteous or indifferent handling of a customer problem, an order canceled because the delivery date was missed?

And the mustard going down the dishwasher's drain represents lost jobs and wages as well as lost profits.

Where Does the Lost Time Go???

"There are no two ways about it," said the plant superintendent in summing up a brass-tacks supervisory meeting he had called on cost control. "We've *got* to pull up slack in our production costs in every conceivable way. Just as your wives have been complaining about skyrocketing prices at the supermarket, our purchasing department has been finding the costs of everything we buy— materials, supplies, and contract services—shooting up. And you all know what the new union contract does to our labor costs.

"The immediate remedy is to get more production out of every productive labor dollar. That means *more standard hours of work per clock hour, less idle time, less waiting time, less overtime, less wasted time.*

"Between now and the next meeting I want all of you to make a concentrated study of *time*. Where does it go? Unproductive time is the one big cost factor under your direct control."

Bart Hewlett took the boss's words to heart. He decided to get some hard facts on lost time in his department. He knew that waiting time occurs primarily because work hasn't been properly planned. True, there was a planning department, but he was responsible for starting the jobs, and he realized that on occasion he was at fault when everything wasn't ready for the operator to get going. And, of course, there were times when delays and down- times were due to factors beyond his own control.

Bart's analysis consisted of making a meticulous, detailed

record of *all* lost time in his department for a period of two hours, at different times, on four different days. His record accounted for every minute of lost time he could notice, or that, on his specific instructions, was reported to him for those test periods.

The results surprised him. In his department of twenty-six men, his eight hours of observation showed that he had lost a total of 1,080 minutes, or an average of 270 minutes per hour. That came to four and a half hours—the equivalent of four and a half men idle for one hour. Assuming that the random scattering of his eight observation hours was representative of what was going on in general in his department, he had to admit to himself that lost time in the department was the same as losing the services of four and a half men all day. That represented over 17 percent of his force!

Of course, not all of the four and a half man-hours per hour lost were within his control or that of his people. But the list was illuminating. It showed that people lost the time because they were waiting for:

Instructions	Maintenance man
Blueprints	Timestudy man
Work order	Crane operator
Tools	Trucker
Material	Toolcrib man
Foreman	Timekeeper
Inspector	Helper
Setup man	Machine availability

Bart had confidence in his ability as a supervisor, and knew that his department operations stacked up among the best in the plant. So he didn't hesitate to discuss his findings with the boss. The superintendent used the figures as prime ammunition at the next supervisory meeting and called for similar breakdowns from all departments. At the same time he kicked off a discussion of measures to take to cut down on the loss.

Not all lost time can be avoided. An alert supervisor, however, like Bart, can greatly cut down on the total once he knows where and why it exists. For example, he will:

- Concentrate on his own planning functions, to be sure no one can hang a delay on him.
- Insist on the necessary planning by individual operators. For example, no more stopping an operation because of running

out of an item of materials or supplies under the operator's control.

- Establish proper communications, so that no unnecessary time is lost waiting for the first piece to be inspected.
- Analyze time lost because of delays of support functions—at the toolcrib, or delays of setup men or maintenance men, or work-order snafus—and take corrective action through proper channels.
- In general, hammer home the slogan, *"Think ahead!"*—not only as regards an individual's planning of his own work, but also stopping to think how an action of his might interrupt the work of somebody else.

In some companies where the above guidelines are closely followed, reports show that avoidable lost time can be brought down to an almost negligible percentage. Try it!

A Switch on Going by the Book

"Keeping score" to pinpoint individual responsibility for supply items will serve to cut down careless wastage, even if no money charges are made against the individuals involved. This idea was put to work by a large drugstore chain when it issued a cost-of-supplies book to all fountain employees, listing the cost of every supply item used in food services at its fountains—every cup and saucer, every dish and glass, and so on.

Whenever a breakage occurred, the employee who had the accident had to turn in a signed memo form that tabulated the name of the article(s) broken, and the cost of the damage to the company based on the figures in the cost-of-supplies book. Although the cost was not charged to the employee, the procedure served to impress everyone with the cost of carelessness. The knowledge that each breakage record was on file tended to make all employees more careful.

The Tale of Two Wastebaskets

"What we should do, Joe," the president of a large insurance company said to the Administrative Services manager, "is to cash in on the resale of our waste paper. Salvage prices have been skyrocketing, I'm told. And with all the talk going around about the need for recycling, we could get some good publicity out of the effort. I know we throw an awful lot of paper away around here."

"But we've instituted a forms-control and stationery conservation program," the A.S. manager replied, quick to go on the defensive.

"I know. I know," said the president, placatingly. "But let's get some dough for what we *do* throw away. So look into it."

Joe did—and found that indeed attractive prices could be obtained for used paper.

But there was a hitch. He found that the key to successful resale of waste paper is proper sorting into appropriate grades, and the removal of contaminants such as paper clips, carbon forms, bottles, and other kinds of waste. With labor costs being what they were, the additional expenditures required for people to do the separating would eat up the profits from the resale. He knew the president wouldn't buy such a program, even with the public-relations mileage to be gained in getting on the recycling bandwagon.

Luckily Joe raised the problem for kicking around at the next day's departmental managers meeting. Young Al Sharpe, from Customer Services, who always seemed to be on the button, had a bright idea. "Why not institute some do-it-yourself salvage screening?" he suggested.

"Like what?" the others wanted to know.

"Well," he said, "a friend of mine with a government job was telling me about a 'separate wastebasket' study being conducted by the United States Public Building Service. It eliminates costly end-of-day separating by putting the burden on individual workers. Everyone gets two or more wastebaskets, earmarked for different types of waste. The clerical people themselves put the bent paper clips and carbons, and things like that, into one basket, and good salvageable stuff in a second basket. Where necessary, a third basket is provided for those high-priced, used IBM cards."

"I owe you a drink, Al," said Joe. "Now I can go to the Old Man not only with a problem, but with a solution!"

The High Cost of "Will Do"

It was late Wednesday afternoon when supervisor Fred Simmons was called into the plant manager's office.

"Fred," said the boss, "here's an inquiry from the Needemfast Company. They want to know whether we can give 'em immediate delivery of 500 out of that run of 5,000 specials scheduled for shipment next month. Can we keep 'em happy by getting those 500 out by Friday night?"

"Will do," said Fred, who liked to think of himself as a do-it-now man.

Fred's department did it all right, even though it played hob with other work, and two of the men had to give up bowling on Thursday night. The shipment to Needemfast went out as promised late Friday night. Fred gave himself a pat on the back.

Two weeks later he was again in the plant manager's office. The boss waved the factory cost report at him before he had a chance to sit down.

"What's all this about cost variances on that Needemfast job? And this overtime! When you said you could schedule the special run, you didn't tell me you meant overtime. Besides which, most of the overtime seems uncalled for in view of the way-below-standard output on the regular shift. And it wasn't even a *must* job. They simply requested the earlier 500 as an accommodation if we could do it."

The sorry facts about the rush job were soon evident from the detailed cost analysis. Fred had given a quick off-the-cuff promise, but when he got back to his department he had found that there were only enough of a certain part to fill 300 of the Needemfast specials order. The other 200 couldn't be obtained until late Friday, which meant Friday overtime.

But there was other bad news. Fred had forgotten that the key man on that particular production line was out that week. A less experienced man had to substitute, and instead of the fifty pieces per hour which was standard for the ticklish Needemfast job, he was only getting forty—which meant overtime had to be scheduled for Thursday. Finally, Fred had also overlooked the fact that one of the machines important for that job was set up for something else. It took four hours to break down the old setup and make a new one (and four hours on Monday to remake the setup for the interrupted job). All in all, the Needemfast job required eighteen hours instead of the ten hours Fred had counted on scheduling for it on Thursday afternoon and Friday.

Could Fred have avoided getting himself into this uncomfortable situation? The answer in this case is obviously *yes*, because he was too quick to say "will do" without knowing his facts, and without finding out whether the boss was willing to incur additional expense. Maybe it would be a good idea for Fred to review some of the following strategy and tactics pointers about rush jobs:

- Be sure your planning gives you maximum leeway. Don't let yourself open to criticism that you can't handle emergencies properly, have unbalanced machine loadings, not enough versatility in personnel, etc. *But—*
- Don't make promises lightly. Know your costs. Develop some cost figures of your own if they are not readily available through normal cost reports. Be prepared to point out to a "rush" requester what the extra costs may be in terms of overtime, special machine setups, premiums for material deliveries, etc. (The requester's enthusiasm may cool when he finds out about the extra dollars involved.)
- Think twice before you "rob Peter to pay Paul." The disruptions and ill will engendered may be out of all proportion to the worth of the rush job. At least, lay the cards on the table at the very beginning.
- Don't sacrifice quality to meet a deadline, without a complete understanding with those for whom you are turning out the work. (Sometimes it is perfectly acceptable to sacrifice some of the icing on the cake in order to get the cake—but don't let the lack of icing come as a surprise!)

"Blow Out the Candle!"

A young man called on a rich old farmer one evening to see if he could learn from him how to become rich.

"It's a long story," said the farmer, "and while I'm telling it, we might as well save the candle." And he blew it out.

"You don't have to go on," said the youth. "I understand."

The Case of the Busted Pipe

Arnold Jenkins, the plant manager, faced his group of operating foremen and his head of Maintenance. He was in an irritable mood because he had just come from a meeting upstairs, where he had been under fire because of high indirect costs.

"Look at these maintenance and emergency repair charges," he fumed, holding up a sheaf of job orders he had earlier pulled out for review. "I've been letting you fellows okay maintenance requests on everything except 'major items,' and I guess I've been too hazy on what is 'major.' From now on, and until further notice, *no* maintenance order will be handled—repeat, *no*—unless it's first approved in this office."

There wasn't much that could be said after that pronouncement so the meeting broke up quickly and everyone went back to work.

But it backfired badly two days later. There was a sudden leak in an overhead water pipe at the end of one of the webbing machines. The foreman of the department, Hank Green, telephoned the maintenance foreman to rush somebody over to repair the leak—it was damaging material coming from the line.

"What d'ya mean, rush over?" said the maintenance foreman. "You heard Arnold—no approved work order, no maintenance work."

Hank pleaded for quick action. More good material was being soaked by the minute. But the maintenance foreman wouldn't budge. He said he didn't make the rule, and Harry shouldn't expect him to break it.

57

After some mad scrambling Hank got the written order and the pipe was fixed, but not before a fair amount of damage was done. As was to be expected, Arnold Jenkins called another meeting—a come-quick one.

There was some tall explaining to do. Arnold grudgingly admitted he had given a flat order, but that here was a case of somebody not using his head. The maintenance foreman started to sputter, but gave up. The atmosphere cooled down, and Arnold admitted that he had to take the blame on this one. Then they all threshed out and agreed to some common-sense rules for operating-department/maintenance-department procedures.

All emergency situations were clearly exempted from the prior work authorization rule, and it was agreed that the operating foremen were to be given leeway in using their own judgment as to what constituted an emergency; no strict rules would be laid down. To guard against a rash of "emergencies," however, *all* such work had to be confirmed by a work order as soon as possible, signed by the plant manager.

Then, a new form for the maintenance work authorization was agreed upon, to be used for routine repairs and improvements as well as emergencies. Enough space was provided for explanatory information in sufficient detail to permit analysis for preventive maintenance records to be built up, and for any subsequent discussion called for. To get Arnold's okay, then, the following would be filled in:

1. *Why must the work be done?* What would happen if it weren't done? Or done in a much simpler way? ("I'm sure that if you have to spell it out in this way," remarked Arnold, "you'll think twice before asking for luxuries and frills.")
2. *How much will it probably cost?* On work of a nonemergency nature, the maintenance personnel would help in arriving at this estimate.
3. *What special advantages are there in doing the work now?*
4. *Comments as required by maintenance foreman.* To be filled in if he has reservations about the need to do the job, or to do it in the way requested, or when requested. (It was assumed that in practically all cases, there would be a meeting of minds between production and maintenance departments before the form was submitted for authorization.)

The Case of the Fancy Stockroom

"You must be out of your mind, Al!"

That was the first reaction of the president of a large cosmetic company after he had listened to the recommendation of his office manager. Al wanted to extend the expensive carpeting of the new headquarters office into the stockroom.

But the president soon changed his mind as he listened to Al's reasoning.

The office manager was able to convince him that by giving the stockroom these "luxurious appointments," as the president had termed them, the company would actually save money. He had recommended the carpeting not out of regard for the appreciation of the finer things of life by the stockroom personnel or because of sound absorption or possible reduction of breakage costs when samples were dropped (although the last two were welcome extras). Al simply presented some figures based on the fact that with this carpeting he would eliminate the last area that would require a mop-and-waxing crew in what was otherwise to be an all-carpeted suite of offices and showrooms.

The savings in these cleaning labor charges would pay for the extended carpeting three times over.

Enemy No. 1: Surprise

"Okay, Ed, all I want are the facts. I guess you know why I'm here, eh?"

"Sure, Bob. I jotted down everything I could pump out of that new man when he jammed the machine—another entry for the 'black book!'"

The day before, Ed had lost a lot of production time in his department when a key machine jammed up. It seemed a clear-cut case of an employee using a wrong speed setting, and neglecting to note the danger signals on machine overload every operator was supposed to keep an eye and ear out for. In this case, the new man claimed he had never been told these particular key points by the assistant foreman, and Ed was going to look into that, as soon as the dislocations of the production foul-up had been taken care of.

In the meantime, following the procedure indicated by the new head of Maintenance, he was giving *all* surrounding details to the assistant maintenance manager, even if some of them reflected on supervision. Under the new system, these details, duly indexed, would go into the now famous "black book."

The book was a comprehensive record the maintenance department was now keeping on *every* kind of mishap and breakdown, including a detailed account of the way emergencies were handled. Already, the ever-growing looseleaf binder, carefully cross-indexed, showed how numerous troublesome situations had been handled, and what changes in procedures or instructions, if any, had been instituted as a result.

"A long time ago," says the head of Maintenance in this large manufacturing plant, "I found that the best way to make a troubleshooting organization function calmly and smoothly is to drill into everyone—the production people as well as my own gang—*Surprise is the enemy of management!*"

The Long and Short of It

"This job certainly wears me out—and yet it isn't really hard. The backs of my legs are killing me!"

"Same here, but it's the bending over that gets me. I've got a crick in my neck right now as though someone had been practicing karate on me."

Foreman Jim Hartung happened to overhear the above conversation between two of his newer women as they walked toward the time clock at the end of one day. It made him think.

He had a large number of women in his department, doing light assembly work. The work required care and patience, but it wasn't—or shouldn't have been—particularly fatiguing. And then he remembered something: Anne, the one who had complained about the backs of her legs, was petite. Louise, who had the crick in her neck, was long-legged and willowy. He had a bright idea, and he asked his assistant, Al Lewis, to work with him after hours a bit, to get moving on it.

The next day the women found the whole department rearranged. All the tall women were now together at their own assembly tables, the medium-sized ones at their tables, and the small ones at theirs. Al Lewis was there to help on making all chair adjustments proper for the new table locations, and Anne's group had a table with shortened legs. Light fixtures, tote-box rests, hanging pneumatically driven screwdrivers, and all other paraphernalia were also carefully adjusted.

Result: No more killing legs, no more cricks.

Nervousness Can Be Contagious!

A large cosmetic company had supplemented its Eastern operations with a new plant in the Midwest. After months of quality problems in the new location, spiraling costs, delays, and back orders, Ted Milner, a long-time foreman in the old plant, was transferred temporarily to the Midwest to help the new manager there (who had been recruited from the outside) to get things rolling.

Ted soon had the production lines humming, and when the president of the company saw the next monthly factory figures, he decided upon a drastic step. He was pretty teed off at the way the new plant had been fouled up. He decided to discharge the new plant manager and jump Ted by a big promotion into the top job.

At the time the decision was being discussed with Ted, an executive from the home office visited the plant. The new zing in operations was immediately apparent to him, since he hadn't been there for several months. He accompanied Ted on a tour through the packaging and filling departments and noticed there weren't any signs of the earlier confusion. At one of the lines, the supervisor mentioned some trouble with bubbles in filling, and Ted had her call the women around him while he explained just how the tricky new cream had to be fed into the jars. Ted knew the operations inside out.

After the plant tour, Ted and the executive stopped into Ted's cubbyhole office for a chat. Ted had this to say: "Yes, I can run the factory operations blindfolded. But this management stuff gets me nervous, even though you fellows say you'll back me up on the cost-accounting and paperwork end. I've been a foreman at the home factory for a long time, but here, with Frank (the ex-manager) gone, I've been 'acting manager,' and now the old man wants me to take on the actual job of running the whole plant."

The executive told him he certainly hadn't seemed nervous in the plant. "You were the picture of confidence and had all the answers. This plant's running like a top."

"Oh," said Ted, "none of the people outside would ever know I'm nervous. I have to let on that everything is under control, no matter how I feel inside. *If I ever let them see I'm nervous, then they would be nervous too!*"

"Ted's definitely the man for the job," the executive reported to the president when he got back to New York.

Work Smarter, Not Harder

As a young engineer at the Bethlehem Steel Company, Frederick W. Taylor, "the father of scientific management," proved that there was a "best way" to do even a simple job like shoveling. (The thought had never occurred to makers or users of shovels before.)

Taylor carefully studied three first-class shovelers, following them around on all of the various materials being handled. He found that a man would do his biggest day's work when the weight of the shovel and load averaged about twenty-one pounds. So he got the company to provide ten different weights and sizes of shovels, earmarked for specific materials, so that the loads would average twenty-one pounds.

Output greatly increased when yard workers used small shovels for heavy ore, and very large ones for light ashes. Previously, a man using the same shovel for all jobs would frequently go from shoveling ore, at about thirty pounds per shovel, to rice coal, with a load on the same shovel of less than four pounds.

*NOTE: The essence of work simplification is the **questioning attitude**. Nothing is taken for granted, and the fact that something has been done in a certain way for a long time is considered to be an argument that there is probably a better way of doing it, not a reason for doing it in that particular way.*

Equate "Safe Way" with "Easy Way"

"Look here, Steve," said the plant superintendent to a supervisor of one of the assembly operations, "the housekeeping in your Framis machine area is terrible—and unsafe. The operators keep dropping finished parts on the floor by their machines, instead of placing them in trays as called for by standard procedures. Their work piles fall over, and you've got a sloppy situation. We keep talking about enforcing the proper work rules. What's the problem here, anyway?"

"I keep telling 'em and telling 'em, Frank," protested Steve. "But they won't take the time for safe practice. Maybe we should take those operators off incentives and put 'em back on day work—and insist on safe procedures."

"And raise all kinds of squawks with them and the union—and cut down on production! Nothing doing," said the boss. "There must be something wrong about that whole operation, or they wouldn't keep treating you that way. First thing tomorrow, shove aside everything else on your docket and take a whole new, fresh look at those jobs. Try some of those work-simplification techniques we've been talking about in those Wednesday sessions. *Make it easy for them to work safely.*"

When Steve took his new look, without any preconceived notions, here is what he found:

- The location of the trays forced the operators to turn partly around in order to place the pieces properly.

- When a tray was filled, an operator had to leave his or her machine to take the tray away and replace it with an empty one. Since the work was on incentive, this was money out of the operator's pocket.
- There was wasted time on the part of the helper whose job it was to carry filled trays to another machine. Lacking sufficient trays, he often had to wait for the operator of the second machine to finish a tray of parts before he could carry the empty back to the first operator. Meanwhile, overloading occurred at the first step, and no empty tray was at hand. The operator *had* to use the floor for temporary storage.

Steve now realized that this was a poorly set-up operation. The safe way was awkward and inconvenient. So he did a little thinking, and then got together with Plant Engineering on the following solution:

- First step was to provide wheeled tray buggies of a height slightly below that of the machine table.
- An inclined slide, or chute, was installed for easy disposal of parts.
- Two buggies with trays were placed in line at a machine, so that when one was filled and the helper was not at hand, the operator simply pushed the filled tray out of the way and pulled the empty one into position, without having to leave his or her work station.
- The chute permitted finished parts to slide down into position without a separate hand-placing operation and without the operator even having to look.

The net result of Steve's study and common-sense moves was more convenience and more production than when pieces were thrown on the floor. So the work was *easier*. And the whole area was *safer* because the danger of accidents from slipping on loose parts on the floor was eliminated.

They Must Be Good— They're Wearing White Gloves!

Colonel Harland Sanders, founder of the nationwide Kentucky Fried Chicken chain and active in the company well into his eighties, journeyed to Lumberton, North Carolina, to present the company's first "White Glove Award" to store owner Edwin Pate of Laurinburg. The award, in the form of a shiny plaque, now hangs in the lobby of the Lumberton KFC outlet, proclaiming it the cleanest in the nation.

The company established the White Glove Award as part of a nationwide cleanliness and sanitation campaign. All of the more than 4,000 franchised and company-owned stores are eligible to compete. "Nothing is more important than a clean store," says KFC president, James H. Wille. "This is an obligation we have to our customers." The purpose of the award is to stimulate all KFC stores to become—and to be recognized as—the cleanest food establishment in their community."

To receive the award, a KFC store must undergo two rigid sanitation inspections at least sixty days apart and achieve no less than a 95 percent rating. Then samples of its chicken and salads are chemically assayed by an independent laboratory to determine microbiological content. The store must receive an "outstanding" rating to pass. If a winning store ever falls below the rigid White Glove standards, the plaque is reclaimed by KFC. The company's field representatives make regular checks to ensure that the standards are maintained. The time lapses required to conduct thorough and accurate White Glove inspections consume more than two months.

Franchise operator Pate had a celebration at his Lumberton store that attracted hundreds of people. In addition to Colonel Sanders, local government and civic leaders attended.

KFC's famous TV commerical jingle is definitely apropos: *"We all can use what the Colonel's got!"*

Cultivate the "Owner's-Eye View"

(The Name of the Game is Profits!)

Do you have the "owner's-eye view" on costs? If so, you're constantly alert to spot avoidable waste—places where profits are dribbling away—whether in your own department or anywhere else in the company.

Example: Luke Sharper, foreman in a company operating a fleet of trucks, happened to be waiting at the company gas pumps for one of the drivers who was going to give him a lift into town. While he was there, a number of trucks drove up for refueling.

Luke noticed that the drivers always filled their tanks to overflowing, allowing excess gas in the hose and nozzle to flow to the ground. He reported his observation to the head of operations.

An immediate directive was issued, correcting the situation.

Result: Estimated savings running into thousands of dollars annually.

The Obvious Deserves Another Look

"What are we gonna do with Joe Brightman, that new job-rotation trainee the v.p. sent down?" the general foreman asked the plant manager.

"I dunno," replied the plant manager. "I'm just too busy this week to line things up for him. But the home office sent him down here to be my assistant for a couple of months. Can you think of some make work for him that will keep him out of my hair for a while?"

"Okay," said the general foreman. "He's supposed to be a bright young industrial engineer. We've been thinking of enlarging our loading dock area. Goodness knows it's pretty jammed up as it is. Why don't I turn him loose on that? He can make some drawings for extending the area, get us cost estimates and things like that, and figure out how much time it'll take to do the modernization. That will keep him busy for a while and who knows, maybe what he comes up with will help us get started on that project at long last."

"Okay," said the plant manager. "Put him on that, and have him check with me on it when I get back from Chicago next week."

When the plant manager got back, he had his secretary locate Joe Brightman and have him come in with his report on the dock project. The plant manager was still up to his ears in work, and had to come to the point right away. "All right, Joe," he said, "let's get to the bottom line right off—how much is that dock extension going to cost us?"

"Nothing, Mr. Bigge," replied Joe.

"What do you mean, nothing?"

"Well, Sir," said Joe, "the way I look at it, we really don't need a dock extension."

"Boy, that's a twist," Mr. Bigge shot back. "For at least a year the boys have been yammering about the clutter out there. And I've seen some of it myself. That dock's always half-loaded with empty drums, scrap, bags of this and that, and trash waiting to be picked up. Al Greene keeps complaining that there's no room for proper storage or staging of orders. There have been plenty of beefs about shipments being held up—"

Joe produced some sketches and laid them on Mr. Bigge's desk. "Here's my idea," he said. "We can easily build a large container with a hinged cover to be located on the north side of the dock. All the refuse and scrap can be dumped into it immediately. Then we can have a special truck come periodically and haul it away, leaving behind another empty container. And as for those drums that have to be saved for reuse or sale, it'll be easy as pie to install a drum rack to free up store space. The way I see it, in this way, we can easily make almost the entire dock area available for its main purpose—efficient shipping."

The plant manager looked at the sketches for a while, and squinted up at Joe. "Pretty good—for a trainee," he said. "Report to Hank Armstrong in Plant Engineering, and tell him I said you and he should implement this idea. In the meantime, I'll give Hank a buzz and make it official." He nodded his dismissal.

Joe left and closed the door behind him, so he didn't hear the plant manager pick up the phone, dial the general foreman, and bark at him, "Ed, I want you and your shipping foreman in this office on the double. You're going to love what I've got to say!"

The Case of the Blind Film Splicers

A few years ago, GAF Corporation, one of the country's largest processors of film, had production problems in its darkrooms. The film splicers had to fumble in the dark, and their output was slow and flawed by errors.

The department manager put up with the situation as best he could, but then one day he had a bright idea: he got the personnel department to hire blind employees to speed operations and eliminate fumbling. He was gratified to find that while employees with normal eyesight could handle 125 rolls of film an hour in the darkroom, the "handicapped" blind could easily better that rate by about thirty-five rolls.

In GAF plants in eight cities, blind darkroom employees were soon opening rolls of film, removing the paper backing on the negatives, splicing the film onto a larger master reel, and inserting the reel into a bag that went to the processing machines.

According to Clarence Colduvell, plant manager at GAF's photofinishing operation in Philadelphia, the reason for the blind employees' success is simple: their sense of touch is incredibly more developed than that of the average sighted person. The blind *must* learn to get information through touch that the rest of us get through vision. "Also," he adds, "they listen for sound cues which have little or no importance to those who have sight. And obvi-

73

ously, they don't lose time 'adjusting' to darkness as they leave and reenter the darkroom with more film."

NOTE the completely reverse thinking: the blind are not the "hand-icapped" in an environment of darkness. The rest of us—the "normal" people—are!

Work-Simplification "Homework"

A consultant in work simplification assigned some homework to the supervisors and department heads of his client company's plant who were enrolled in his work simplification seminar. After his first introductory session on the breakdown of an operation into its elements for analysis, he asked them to draw up a detailed listing of *all* the steps they went through when they shaved themselves the next morning.

All of the separate elements were to be described broken down in terms of walking, reaching, grasping, moving an object from one location to another, the "value-adding operation" of "scraping face," etc. He also asked them to have an electric clock in view so that they could get a record of the time taken on each.

The men entered into the spirit of the thing, and at the next session came up with some composite experiences of direct application to departmental operations. One man's "scrape face" took unconscionably long, because his blade was extremely dull and he didn't have a replacement (*poor planning*). Another had difficulty in getting his shaving cream from amongst a lot of miscellaneous items in the medicine cabinet, and had knocked over and broken a bottle of his wife's lotion in the process (*poor make-ready*). Another had found that he'd forgotten to take the blade out of his razor the last time he'd shaved, and had a sticky mess to clean up before he could get started (*poor put-away*). Several discovered that because they were still sticking with the old brush-and-lather method, they were

75

averaging from 50 to 100 percent more time than the others (*failure to use known faster devices*).

One bright young engineer came in with a detailed analysis of the total time he would save during the year, if he invested in the most expensive long-lasting blades, and was surprised to learn that not only was he wasting considerable time with the less efficient blades, but that his straight out-of-pocket cost per shave was actually higher with the less expensive blade (*sound through-put analysis*).

Al Ferguson Uses Psychology

Al Ferguson ran a sheet-metal and air-conditioning contracting firm. He had some seventy men out in the field on a dozen different installation jobs at any given time, and was going over an accumulation of purchase orders. Suddenly he came across one of them that made him yelp and reach for the phone to dial his construction supervisor. "Jim," he said, "can you come in here PDQ?! I want to discuss this order for Frobish fittings."

Jim came in. The call wasn't entirely unexpected. "So you're wondering about that order I put through for the couplings, eh?" he said.

"Wondering!" exclaimed Al. "That's a mild word for it! I distinctly remember okaying an order for 40,000 of those just last month. I've got Martha looking up the papers."

"No need for her to search the files," countered Jim. "I pulled the carbons myself when I put through this new order. The fact is, we're practically out of them and we've got to have 'em. The boys apparently have been using 'em up pretty fast—"

"You can say that again," said Al. "I really don't see how they could have used up 40,000 since that last order even if they sat on the tailgates of the trucks and threw them out on the streets!"

"Al, I know how you feel," said Jim. "But it's pretty tough to control supply items like that. We load the trucks each morning for the various jobs and keep them all supplied with the hardware needed. If I began asking the journeymen to sign out individual requisition slips by job number for every conceivable item, with carbons for my office and Accounting and Purchasing and then tried

77

to set up a control procedure for usage—often unpredictable—against budgets for jobs, we'd all soon be drowning in paperwork. And I can't run a stores department on each truck, with a stores clerk collecting and sorting requisitions for each item taken. And don't forget, every man on the truck has to be a journeyman or apprentice, or a full-fledged union man—and you know what the new union hourly wages are. Any decent paperwork control would cost even more than the Frobish fittings, to say nothing of the other items."

"Look, Jim," said Al. "I know the problem, but let's try a little psychological control."

"How do you mean—psychological?"

"Fix up a simple sign-off log sheet," Al explained. "When a guy takes supplies from the truck, have him sign the sheet, with an abbreviated notation for what he took and the amount."

"You mean a snap-out carbon form, in triplicates?" asked Jim.

"No, no duplicates or triplicates," countered Al, "and no pink or yellow copies for Accounting or Purchasing or anyone else."

"Oh, I see," said Jim, "you'll have Martha make the usage analysis."

"No," said Al, "nobody's going to make any analysis. You can dispose of the filled-in log sheets in your circular file. I'm counting on the psychology of the thing. Just start the procedure off, and let's see how long this new 40,000 will last. Tell the boys it's a special running audit we're doing on a temporary basis for tax purposes. It'll work, I'm sure."

Jim tried it, and it worked. A month went by and there was only a mild dent in the supply of Frobish fittings in inventory.

"All right, Jim," said Al, after seeing how things were going. "Call off that sign-off log sheet procedure. You can tell the fellows that our spot-audit procedure for tax purposes is finished. If I get jolted again by a Frobish fitting or whatever purchase order, we can always reinstitute it."

"Hooray for psychology!" said Jim.

The Horrible "As Is"!

The story is told of Frank Gilbreth, the famous motion-and-time study expert, taking a flow-process chart into the office of a plant executive of a client company. He unrolled the chart for inspection and it stretched clear across the office.

"See here, Gilbreth," the executive exploded. "Roll that damned thing up and take it out of here. I don't know what it is, but I don't have to know, because I'm against it!"

"But Mr. Blank," said Gilbreth, "this isn't any proposal that I am making. It's only an exact representation of the flexo-grimping process as it already exists in your plant." He then unrolled a small, three-and-a-half-foot flow-process chart drawn to the same scale. *"Here's the proposed method,"* he said.

How They Saved McNulty's Job

"I want to take Tim McNulty back," said the plant superintendent to Tim's foreman, Art Nash. "You know darn well that none of the replacements we've tried has been satisfactory. Good crane operators in Tim's job grade are hard to find."

"Sure, I'd like to take him back too," replied Art. "He came to see me yesterday. But you know what the doc said. What can I do? It's tough on Tim and tough on us—but my hands are tied."

The plant processed slag, a residue from iron-melting operations. Tim's job had been to operate an electric locomotive crane to load and unload various sizes of slag aggregates on and off open-top railroad cars. Unfortunately, he had developed a painful skin disease on his legs and thighs; he lost strength and found it difficult to stand for any length of time. He had been taken off the job for twenty-one weeks, but now was pretty well recovered. But the plant doctor said that at fifty-six years of age, and after the siege he had been through, he'd never be able to stand the physical strain of the crane operator's job. He recommended reassignment to a lower-paying but less demanding job.

But quite aside from personal considerations (Tim had been with the company for twenty-five years), the superintendent just couldn't afford to lose him as a crane operator. "Wait a minute, Art," he said. "we can't redesign Tim McNulty, but I'm sure that we can redesign that job to bring it within doc's stipulations. Besides, all the other jobs I could use him on also require a lot of standing. Suppose you get together with Plant Engineering and Maintenance, take a good look at Tim's operations and equipment, and come back with some answers.'

The job analysis showed that there was indeed a great deal of physical effort in that crane operation. To enter, Tim had been climbing a short stepup ladder. He had to push and pull three long-handled levers to actuate the booms and hoists. And to move the locomotive crane forward and back (using third-rail power) involved two friction-clutch foot brakes on which Tim had to put his full body weight while standing. There was a stool in the cab, but Tim could seldom sit down on it; in his work, he had to "fight the machine all day," since there was only one electric locomotive crane in the plant yard.

Here's what Art Nash and Plant Engineering and Maintenance came up with—and at a cost of only $750:

They made it easy to enter the cab from the platform at the starting station, so that the step-up ladder had to be used only infrequently. They installed easily operated mechanical foot brakes and pneumatic controls in place of the manually operated foot brakes and long-handled mechanical controls. Tim could now work air-powered levers and valves while sitting down most of the time, to work the clamshell buckets and to move the crane along the track.

Result: One good crane operator back on the job. The controls were different, but Tim could perform the same operations he always did, in the same job classification, and at the same pay.

SCENARIO 36

Battle of the Sexes

How do male employees react to having a woman supervisor? Barbara Blakney, a production supervisor at RJR Archer, Inc., Winston-Salem, N.C., has some answers to that question. Blakney started with the company as a clerk-typist, but after a stint at that she requested to move to the factory floor. "I thought it would be more of a challenge," she explains.

At time of interview, Barbara was supervising eighteen men and ten women in the finishing and material-flow department. "When I got the job, I saw mixed reactions from the people I worked with," she remembers. "One male employee came right out and told me that he didn't like working for a woman because he had been bossed all his life by women—first by his mother, then his wife."

Barbara's answer to that was, "I'm another employee, just like you, performing a job just like you. When I do my job, that involves asking you to do yours." (He shaped up.)

The Blakney formula for being a successful woman supervisor is learning to be aware of her employees' individuality, whether men or women. "I make a point of stopping by to talk with each of my employees," she says. "You can learn a lot from reading between the lines—that is, *listening* between the lines—in a casual conversation.

Her postscript: "I'd like to see more women come into the industrial field and see what it's like. I think they would have more pride in the company they work for if they were involved in industrial operations."

82

The Case of the Workers Who Minded Their Own Business

"There's something basically wrong over at the Zilch Company," said consultant John Sweeney, shaking his head and signalling the waiter for another drink. "And," he added, "there's nothing I can do about it as an industrial engineer—it goes deeper. It has to do with all kinds of things like climate, inspiration by supervisors, top management attitude, and so on."

Sweeney was comparing notes after hours with a colleague, about their client, the Zilch Company, which had engaged their firm to put in production standards and controls and in general to tighten up on productivity.

"How do you mean that?" his associate wanted to know.

"It's hard to put your finger on exact causes," Sweeney replied. "But here's a for instance:

"You know the problem they've been having about poor quality and customer returns. Well, they've got a job going through the shop for one of the space subcontractors, and everybody by now should know how critical *their* tolerances are.

"One of the components calls for turning out thousands of a set of fittings. Nothing complicated—part A has to screw snugly into part B. It happens that the fellow turning out part A works on a machine side by side with the fellow turning out part B on another machine. I happened to be in the department just before closing this afternoon, and on an off-hand impulse I picked up a part A and tried to screw it into part B. It didn't go in!. I picked up a few more, at random, with the same result. No fit.

"Naturally, I immediately got hold of the supervisors and the plant manager, and the big flap began. They shut down the line immediately, and began checking blueprints and specs and machine settings and the whole bit. And, of course, also wrote out some tickets for scrap counts and rework.

"But what gets me," Sweeney concluded, "is that here these two guys had been working side by side for a day and a half on a job they should have known was important—and they should have known that they were both working on the same component. But at no time during that day and a half had either of them been interested enough to pick up a couple of pieces and see if they did indeed screw together."

"I see what you mean," said Sweeney's sidekick. "We'd better do some talking *upstairs* at Zilch's tomorrow."

The Boss Who Threw Money Away

A story told by Lee Grossman in his book, *The Change Agent* (American Mangagement Associations), has it that there was an owner of a small manufacturing business who was troubled because nuts, bolts, and assorted small parts were always left lying on the factory floor. One day he walked into the center of the assembly area, took out a roll of dimes, unwrapped it, and tossed the coins into the air. He watched while they rolled every which way, then calmly turned around and walked back to his office, leaving the assemblers and foreman to pick up the dimes, shaking their heads and saying that it was too bad, but the boss had obviously gone off his rocker.

The next day the owner called a meeting of all assembly area employees. "By now you're wondering what made me throw money around the assembly floor," he said. "No, I'm not off my rocker. I was simply trying to impress you with the fact that we have a problem.

"Every day when I come out to the manufacturing area and to the assembly area I see assorted parts lying on the floor and notice that nobody bothers to pick them up. *But those parts represent money out of my pocket!* Every time you fail to pick up a nut or bolt or carelessly drop some cotter pins you are throwing money away. Yes, I threw money away yesterday—but those dimes were no more *real* money than the parts and supplies you're wasting every day. As a matter of fact, in these days of inflation, those dimes, sad to say, are getting to be worth less every day, whereas the items you're overlooking are getting to be worth *more* all the time!

"End of meeting."

Get Everyone into the Act

The president of a large corporation which had experienced a sharp drop in earnings received the following letter from an obscure employee in a branch location:

> I would like to make a suggestion on how to save the Company some money. I think you should start a campaign with publicity in the various plant employee newspapers, on bulletin boards, etc., entitled *"What Did I Do Today to Save the Company Money?"* In this way, employees throughout the organization could be made aware of their fellow employee's ideas to help the company's financial situation.
>
> I'm thinking of small things such as recycling extra forms supplies. (Many of our employees still discard extras rather than send them to supply rooms.) . . . Or reducing reproduction costs by making carbon copies instead of Xeroxes where only one or two extras are needed and by not making more copies than needed.
>
> The above are just two examples. If every employee did his part to save money, things might look a little brighter in the future.

The significance of the letter, which was acknowledged with thanks and *acted upon*, was not in the specific savings suggested, but in the fact that it showed that everyone could be brought into the cost-cutting act. The suggested campaign was launched, with bulletin-board and employee publication, and special-meeting publicity. While at this writing it was still too early for a dollars-and-cents recap, the nature and range of suggestions received are impressive: at company headquarters, some employees agreed to start work early, and others to stay late, to make better use of the long-distance WATS service. Some purchasing operations were centralized to get better volume price breaks. One employee's suggestion to use aluminum instead of copper for a certain product part netted a $485,000 saving. Executives agreed to fly tourist class instead of first class on business trips. A requisitioning improvement substantially reduced average supplies inventory. Numerous forms were combined into one, saving on forms printing and inventory. And so on.

What did *your* department do to save money today?

A parting thought on operations

You ask me, do we still keep a sharp eye on costs? Always.
You can never relax on that. My father taught me a little
lesson about it. He was in Europe when we had our first
$10,000 day at the F&R Lazarus store in Columbus. I was so
proud I sent him a cable to break the news. He sent me con-
gratulations, but did not cable them. He wrote me, saying
that he, too, was very proud, and added, "But couldn't you
have written and not spent the money for a cable?"

—*Fred R. Lazarus, Jr.*

PART THREE

CHECK

What Accounting and Budgeting Are All About

(In One Easy Lesson!)

In one of the plants of a large instrument manufacturing company, a seminar on budgeting and standard costs was arranged. At the opening session, the head of the cost engineering department was asked to give the kick-off talk.

He held up one of the company's products. "I suppose you know what this is," he said. "Sure!" "Of Course!" "Naturally," were the immediate responses, with a chorus—"A *thermocouple*."

"I see you know your own business," said the cost executive. "Now how about this one?" and he held up another one of the company's well-known devices.

"A *thermostat*," came the immediate shout.

"Right again," said the cost engineer. "And now you know what accounting and budgeting are all about. This thermocouple, selling for hundreds of dollars, is a *measuring* instrument. It merely tells us what is going on. Accounting does the same.

"The thermostat—and incidentally, the one I showed you sells for just a few dollars—is a *control* instrument. It not only tells us what is going on, but keeps the temperature within a given range. That's what budgeting does.

"Now all we have to do during the rest of this seminar is fill you in on some of the details!"

93

SCENARIO 41

Red Tape . . .
or Road Map?

"If you ask me," grumbled Steve Hardy to the general foreman as they filed out of the monthly factory cost meeting held in the plant manager's office, "there's getting to be too darn much paperwork in this shebang. I'll bet I know more about widgets—at least about our operations on 'em—than anyone in the company. But when they made me foreman, I didn't think I'd be buried in paper, and have to worry about all these percentages and variances and what-have-you. Maybe they were looking for an accountant, and not a widget expert!"

"Hold on a minute, Steve," said general foreman Harry Beggs. "You're fighting 'em when you should be *joining* 'em. You're part of management now, and not just a widget expert. These variance reports you're getting are the best *management tool* you've got. I know you've had a lot of new stuff thrown at you since you took over that department, and I don't blame you for sounding a bit frustrated. Stop in my office a minute and we'll go over last month's report step by step."

Let's follow them into Beggs' office, and look over their shoulders as Beggs explains, "Departmental Variance Report—Dept. 10." The variance report is shown in the accompanying exhibit. Like Steve Hardy, we'll find that this advanced-practice type of departmental cost analysis is quite easy to understand, and certainly gives a clear picture as to whether operations in Department 10, Wigdets, are proceeding according to plan.

94

DEPARTMENTAL VARIANCE REPORT

CURRENT MONTH			ITEMS	
		26,400	Budgeted Standard Productive Hours	
		29,040	Accounted Standard Productive Hours	
		110%	Department Activity	
VARIANCE FOR MONTII ( ) = red ink	ACTUAL	CURRENT ALLOW- ANCE	ACCOUNT	
			No.	NAME
(1,270)	$88,390	$87,120	8.1	DIRECT LABOR
			8.2	PRODUCTION MATERIALS
				DIRECT OVERHEAD
	1,250	1,250	9.1	Chief Foreman's Salary
	1,800	1,800	9.2	Assistant Foremen's Salaries
(452)	8,912	8,460	9.3	Indirect Labor
(420)	5,956	5,536	9.4	Spoiled Work
52	2,448	2,500	9.5	Perishable Tools
656	2,104	2,760	9.6	Manufacturing Supplies
110	1,670	1,780	9.7	Power
(50)	24,136	24,086		TOTAL OVERHEAD
(1,320)	112,526	111,206		TOTAL DEPARTMENT
REMARKS				
DEPARTMENT 10			MONTH: March	
DEPARTMENTAL OPERATING REPORT				

Note that "standard productive hour" is used as a measure of volume of production. All Steve Hardy has to keep in mind is that a standard productive hour is a measure of work produced that is of acceptable quality. Thus, if the standard time developed by the fellows over in the methods department calls for 2.0 minutes for a piece, then thirty pieces produced would be the equivalent of producing "one standard productive hour's worth of work." Since the quantities of the various pieces going through Steve's department are budgeted ahead of time, at the time the plant's yearly budget is made up, the aggregate of work to be done can be translated into terms of "standard productive hours" on the basis of the specific standard time set for each type of piece worked on.

The exhibit shows how a report would be presented to Steve for the month of March. Note that a certain number of productive hours of work had been budgeted for that month. However, because of a sales spurt beyond the original budget, the department actually produced 29,040 standard hours instead of the budgeted 26,400, giving a "Department Activity" of 110 percent for the month.

Steve's company is working under a flexible budget system. That means that for a wide range of possible levels of activity, the accounting department had precalculated what the budgeted costs should be at any given level for direct labor, production materials, and all overhead items. Therefore, in the column headed "Current Allowance," there are figures entered showing what Steve was "allowed" to spend *at the 110 percent level of activity* for March—the level at which his department actually worked, rather than the originally budgeted level.

At this point, Harry spreads out for Steve the detailed "Departmental Flexible Budget" for his department, showing the budgeted allowances for all of the items listed on the March report, at five percentage point step intervals for activity ranging from 70 percent of "normal" through 125 percent. (March happened to be a month budgeted at "Normal." Because of expected seasonal fluctuations, other months are budgeted at other levels.)

Of course, in real life you never hit the budget right on the nose. Therefore, in the column headed "Actual" are entered all of the *actual* costs incurred in Steve's department in March, shown alongside the "allowed" costs. The differences between the actual and the allowed costs are entered in the "Variance" column. Unfavorable results are shown in parentheses. Similarly shown are the results for the year to date.

Such a report pinpoints results quite finely, and enables Steve to spot "sore thumbs," which he will have to explain at the monthly cost meeting in the manager's office.

As Steve and Harry discuss this report, what are some of the causes that could have given rise to the variances shown? There is an adverse variance in direct labor. This could have been due to untrained help whose performance fell below the standards set. Or there may have been absences on a conveyor line so that the line could not be properly balanced as regards manning, in accordance with engineered methods, resulting in reduced output per worker on the line. Or Steve's planning could have been at fault, resulting in downtime while there was a wait for materials or supplies, again cutting down on expected output per direct man-hour.

Production materials are distinguished from supplies, which are part of overhead. In this report, there is no entry in this space, because Steve's department is merely working on pieces received from another department, and the spoiled work account would reconcile discrepancies.

In Steve's report there is no variance for the chief foreman's or the assistant foreman's salaries.

The indirect-labor variance could have been caused by some extra demands by Steve's department for work by setup men or adjusters, and the spoiled work could have been due to untrained help. On the other hand, his people used fewer supply items (safety gloves, lubricants, and the like), and the power bill was less than budgeted.

"From now on, Steve," says Harry as he closes his binder of collected cost reports, "you're going to play a direct part in this 'numbers game.' At the beginning of the budget period, the people from Cost Accounting will be over to get your opinion before developing figures on such items as the amount of indirect labor (material handling, maintenance, and so on) that should be allocated to your operations for various levels of production. They'll discuss direct-labor allowances with you, so that you'll have a say as to whether certain high levels of production would call for budgeting overtime, for transfers-in from some other department, or perhaps for new hires. You'll also have a part in determining the direct-labor hours needed because of your day-by-day knowledge of methods improvement made or to be made in your department, and other cost-reduction ideas you may have.

"So—what do you think of the system now?"

"Looks like a darn good road map," says Steve. "I'm through fightin'. I'm gonna *join* 'em!"

You Can't Tell Time with a Busted Watch!

Jim Bledsoe, a foreman in a machinery manufacturing company, took his monthly cost reports seriously—always checking his department's performance against standards, and trying to come up either with reasonable explanations or corrective action when results were out of line.

But the scrap account bothered him, and frustrated him. He had complained several times at cost-variance meetings that he felt his scrap allowance was too low. For several months in a row he'd miss it (on the wrong side) by wide margins, but he didn't seem to have any "handle" on the problem. Then, unaccountably, in the last report he was way *under* the budgeted scrap losses.

But instead of basking in some long-delayed glory for good results, Jim decided to raise the whole question again, and in stronger terms, because they showed him to be *too* good. "This is like trying to tell time with a busted watch," he said. "There *has* to be something wrong with the standards."

It was good that Jim (no accountant himself) insisted that in this case the cost accountants were at fault. Like all companies in his industry, Jim's company was always confronted with a serious scrap control problem, and Jim's beefing about his individual department's "report card" triggered a full-scale investigation into the way the allowances were arrived at.

The cost engineers used Jim's department as a sample, and made a detailed study of all his scrap charges, going back a year. It turned out that on an overall basis, the allowance as set for the twelve months just about matched the level of scrap he actually incurred. But not on a *monthly* basis. For this, depending on volume of operations and the kind of work being done, it was sometimes too high, and sometimes too low. Definitely, the monthly cost information Jim was getting on scrap was nothing he could use intelligently in his own departmental control.

Further study (including other departments) clearly showed the reason for the fluctuations. Departmental scrap allowances had been set at so much per departmental direct production hour at a time when the company's products were much less diversified. Investigation of Jim's operations, for example, disclosed widely varying scrap generation, depending on product tolerances, design specifications, and other factors. One product might result in ten times as much scrap, proportionately, as another. The monthly total depended entirely on the products that happened to be passing through his department.

The investigation occasioned by the persistence of a single departmental supervisor sparked a full-scale industrial-engineering study which had as its objective the development of *meaningful* scrap allowances by *part*, monthly *departmental* scrap allowances based on forecast production, and sufficient analysis of scrap to disclose parts and operations in which *scrap incidence* was high.

Over 30,000 scrap tickets were analyzed by job number, department, and operation. Scrap percentages were calculated in two ways: (1) number of pieces scrapped compared with quantity shipped, and (2) cost of scrap on each part as a percentage of aggregate manufacturing cost.

At meetings with departmental supervisors, these results were reviewed and tentative standards by part were agreed to. (These were on the whole lower than past departmental standards, in line with a drive to achieve reduction in total scrap costs.) Monthly scrap reports were then issued, clearly pinpointing peformance against standards by part and operation, broken down for major jobs in each department.

The foregoing results were highly satisfactory as far as they went. But the whole problem aired by Jim's original complaint was now one of engrossing interest to the cost experts and to top operating management. They saw that the new information was now meaningful, but that a lot more should be done as to its *timeliness*. They liked Jim's reference to the need for a good watch, but they wanted their scrap readings to be taken closer than once a month, with a reporting time lag added on.

The result was a radical departure calling for scrap reporting on a *daily* basis, using advanced equipment to transmit scrap information to the company's computer center and to receive it back on tapes convertible to reports on scrap by "pieces, cost, and operations responsible" for the supervisor's desk when he arrived at work each morning.

With that one under control, Jim is now looking at other problems.

Understanding Management's Balancing Act

In 1859 the French tightrope walker and acrobat, Jean François Blondin, created a worldwide sensation by crossing Niagara Falls on a strand of wire 11,000 feet long, stretched 160 feet above the water. For good measure he did the stunt a number of times, always with different theatrical variations: blindfolded, in a sack, trundling a wheelbarrow, on stilts, carrying a man on his back, and sitting down midway while he made and ate an omelette. (No slips: he lived to a ripe old age.)

While not so spectacularly as Blondin, the management of the average company must continuously do a balancing act of its own to keep the business afloat and prosperous. The result of bad decisions can directly affect the welfare of many more people (employees, shareholders, creditors) than could a tragic misstep by Blondin, with all his cheering thousands of onlookers. Management must walk a tightrope between aggressively going after markets, and overextending itself in credit, advertising, and promises to customers; between prompt customer service, and tying up too much money in inventory; between being competitive with the best in equipment and facilities, and having too much of its assets frozen in machines and bricks and mortar; between hanging on to its working force when in the red, and being unprepared when the upturn comes because the axe was swung for economy's sake.

101

But these are management's headaches—why tell departmental supervisors about them? In Joseph Conrad's phrase, they are part of the "privileges and reponsibilities of command," and establishing policy on them is beyond the supervisor's province. But it is well for the supervisor to realize the kind of problems that must be coped with outside the four walls of his own department. Thus he may have a clearer notion of why the front office didn't okay that requisition for the "measly 450 bucks" to buy a piece of equipment that would save time and cut down bottlenecks in his department. Or why he can't get that assistant to free himself from so much paperwork. Or why the company decided not to go ahead with plans for that new plant after all.

No supervisor is expected to be a trained accountant unless he or she happens to be supervisor in an accounting department. But to understand why certain reports are required of him—or why so much to-do is made of indirect costs in his department, or how it happens that his department is "overabsorbing" or "underabsorbing" overhead, or what it is that the company is trying to say in its explanations of its "simplified" annual statements issued to employees—it is worthwhile for him at least to acquire an understanding of the terms that are commonly used, and of some of the underlying concepts on which management's accounting and budgetary controls are based. (But take a look at the next scenario, too.)

Take control reports seriously. If you don't understand what some of the figures mean, and wonder how they were arrived at, ask questions.

"Is This Report Necessary?"

A story has it that a top executive, seeing the avalanche of data pouring out of his data-processing center, selected a computer printout page at random, and wrote on it: "I will pay $1,000 to anyone who sees this message and calls me." No one called.

The story is undoubtedly fictitious, but it makes a point for all managers. Most common computer printers in use today can print over 1,100 lines a minute, or roughly 32,000 pages of single-space output a day. The problem today is often not that there isn't *enough* information for management decisions and control, but that there is simply *too much*.

Every executive, from the supervisor on up, has to contend with apparently ever-increasing paperwork. Here are some questions to ask about reports routinely received from Accounting, Production Control, Sales Analysis, and other sources of information: Do they give you significant information quickly, without your having to leaf through pages of data? Do they get to you in time to take effective action? Would fewer, timelier reports be of more value? Or less frequent reports with a smaller time lag?

Of course, an individual departmental manager or suprvisor may have little directly to say about the format, coverage, and frequency of most of the reports coming to him. But only by analyzing their usefulness and making your views known to the originating departments will you ever effect an improvement. And don't forget to look closely at reports prepared within you own department, for your own managerial purposes as well as for your superiors and for other groups. Is the time spent by you and others in recording raw data and preparing and checking the final reports justified by the use you and others make of the results?

Are You Driving Blind?

Hal Winters was driving to work on a certain morning, as he did every working day, when he suddenly noticed that the fuel indicator on the dashboard was at the very bottom "below zero" point on the dial. "Holy Smoke," he said to himself, "I'm sure I filled the tank just the other day! And it's miles to the nearest gas station."

Luckily he made it to the station under the car's own power. But then Al Boulding, who was running the pumps, had news for him. "You only needed two gallons, Hal," he said.

Investigation showed that the gauge wasn't working, and Hal made arrangements for someone to drive him to the plant while he left the car to be repaired.

"Sure gives you a nervous feeling," Hal reflected, "having no feedback to tell you how much gas you've got left in your tank and how fast you're using it up." And then it suddenly dawned on him that in his own department at the plant, and probably in a good many others too, there were operations that were running "without a gas gauge," with no feedback on how energy and supplies were being used, and how much, if any, was being wasted.

In Hal's department there was a "steam-stripping column"—an apparatus used to remove volatile impurities from a liquid. The column was designed to operate on 14,000 pounds of steam an hour. But there was no flow meter on the incoming steam line, and Hal now saw that all the time the apparatus had been there, no one could tell just how much steam was actually being used. The operators were just opening the valve three of four turns, making sure that the product was all right, and letting it go at that.

At Hal's suggestion, Plant Engineering spent several thousand dollars opening up the line and installing the needed flow meter. As it turned out, the actual use had been 10,000 pounds an hour—3,000 more than was needed for the process. At the price the plant was paying for steam, cutting back on the flow reduced the annual steam bill by $30,000.

Hal had some other ideas about measuring for feedback, but they went beyond his own department. So he brought the matter up at that week's supervisory meeting. With costs of energy and supplies skyrocketing, the possibilities were immediately apparent and the plant superintendent ordered a plantwide "What Can We Measure for Savings?" program.

Some Immediate Measures

- Power was metered to all "cost centers" for direct allocation of charges, instead of the former accounting department pro-rating system. Departmental managers were told that detailed charge-backs would be made. *Result:* along with a "turn off power and lights when not in use" campaign, power consumption was cut by an amount that almost equaled the steep rise in utility rates caused by the oil crisis.
- To ensure minimal use of air conditioning consistent with reasonable comfort and efficiency, time clocks were installed on all individual units in use.
- Automatic shut-off devices were put on all pump nozzles in the company garage to eliminate the waste of gas when company trucks and cars were fueled. *Result:* study of cost-accounting records showed that the seemingly insignificant wastage now recovered enabled one of the trucks to operate on half of its runs "for free."
- All copy machine were equipped with counters and key-operated controls, with costs strictly logged against code-identified users. *Result:* the time-honored "government work"—personal jobs, bridge scores, club announcements, etc.—was eliminated.
- Postage meters and accurate weighing devices were installed in the mail room. *Result:* not only more accurate accounting for postage, with no more "borrowing" of stamps, but also accurate postage amounts on all outgoing mail, at a significant saving.

- But a big saving from "measured feedback" didn't involve any instrumentation at all. As a result of Hal's suggestion, one of the supervisors recommended that they should see what could be saved by a real measurement of *scrap losses*. The supervisor, Jim Bledsoe, reported that while he was keeping within preset limits on a yearly basis, the monthly fluctuations, he found, varied widely. Jim made a "quickie" study in his department, and found that the variations depended on product tolerances, design specifications, and other factors. (For what he did about it, see Scenario 42.)

Giving Rejects the Air

"Look, Bill," said the plant superintendent, "how come the records show that your department has a rejects and mistakes record almost 20 percent higher than Nate Harder's department on the floor below you? You're both doing the same type of work, and on the average you have the same number of people reporting to you. Talk to Nate. Look into what may be wrong."

Bill and Nate made a careful checkup. Analysis showed that performance of Bill's group was consistently poorest from the middle of the afternoon on. One of the workers suggested that something be done about ventilation. By the time 2:30 came around, she said, the poor air in the place gave her a headache.

A simple, inexpensive ventilation installation did the trick—a short run of the ductwork and a blower. "We gave the rejects the air," Bill was able to report to the boss.

Don't Underestimate the Value of a Score Card

"They're doing something over at XYZ Company, where my brother-in-law works, that might be a good idea here," Chuck Davis remarked during the course of a supervisors' meeting.

"What's that?" asked the plant manager.

"Harry, my brother-in-law, calls it 'the power of publicity,'" said Chuck.

"They post their daily performance records. Harry claims these posted records are a big psychological incentive to get people who are performing below standard up to standard and over. They don't dock the pay of the guys and gals who fall below standards; but the supervisors single them out for special coaching."

"What kind of records do they post?" asked one of the other supervisors at the meeting.

"Well," explained Chuck, "they've got a standard-minute incentive over there—something like our own performance-standards system. They knew that the bonus incentive itself would step up productivity. But they found that they gave the financial incentives a big boost when they began posting a daily production report in a prominent place in each department.

"It's a simple report, listing department employees by name, together with the standard minutes produced the previous days, and their earned bonus. The figures are easily put together from the timestudy department records. But the important thing, says Harry, is that the names are listed in the order of performance—highest on top.

"Everyone wants to rate high on the list—and hopefully to be first. They like the bonus money, of course, but they also like to show up well in front of the whole department.

"Incidentally, Harry says that posting is an incentive to supervisors also—when the plant manager walks through the department, the first thing he does is go to the bulletin board to see the latest performance score."

"Let's give the idea a whirl," said the plant manager. "I like all the reasons—especially that last one!"

How Good Is 100 Percent Good?

Ken Nickerson had promised to cooperate with an outside consultant who had been brought in to install SQC—statistical quality
control. But he couldn't help having strong reservations when
sampling techniques were substituted for 100 percent inspection.
The consultant talked a lot about "normal curves," "histograms,"
"frequency distributions," and "control charts," but Ken wondered
aloud how anything could ever be more reliable than 100 percent
checking of all pieces produced, or pieces bought from vendors.

"I'll show you how good your hundred-percent inspection is,"
said the consultant, and he gave him a card with a single sentence
on it. "Block-letter this sentence on index cards, and pass them out
to twenty or twenty-five people in your department," he said. The
card read: FEDERAL FUSES ARE THE RESULT OF SCIEN-
TIFIC STUDY COMBINED WITH THE EXPERIENCE OF
YEARS.

"Ask the people you give the cards to, to pretend that the letter
F is a defective part," said the consultant. "Twenty seconds ought
to be enough time for this check. Then tally the results, and compare them with the true number."

Ken did so, and found that only four out of his group had the
right answer, even though there were only seventy-three letters in
the whole sentence! (As a matter of fact, when he had tried it out
on himself, he had come up with a figure of seventy-two.)

The consultant gave Ken another card, with the instruction,
"Read the three phrases on this card out loud—right off the
bat—and then read them again, to yourself, carefully." Here is
what was on the card—try it yourself:

NOTE: Results such as the above should indicate that 100 percent inspection is by no means insurance that all defects will be found. Thus, quite apart from the cost, complete inspection of every part in a lot is a poor way of finding out if all of them meet specifications. As a matter of fact, 100 percent inspection is not "total inspection." To approach total inspection, one has to conduct 100 percent checking more than once—a few times, or great many times, depending upon conditions. Operator fatigue has an important effect on inspection, as do factors such as interruptions and distractions, the type of gauging being done, working conditions in general, the frame of mind of the inspector, and so on. As more and more pieces of the same kind are inspected in the same way, monotony begins to play a part, causing carelessness and perhaps drowsiness.

Thus it can be seen that careful inspection of samples, if done according to calculated risks based on probability theory, will actually provide more assurance than 100 percent final inspection. Experience has shown that 100 percent final inspection is definitely less than 100 percent reliable, especially if defects are to be caught by ordinary visual observation. For this reason, within-process 100 percent inspection is more reliably replaced by evaluation of finished lots by means of well-known sampling procedures (probability sampling by variables) to give adequate assurance that the finished lot meets quality specifications.

Of course, quality cannot be inspected into a product or service; it must be an integral part of the overall design and production operation. After the designers and engineers have done their part, it is up to supervisors to see that the people on the job are fully quality conscious and are doing their part to hold down rejects and scrap.

Psychological Surveillance

In his "Short Course for Foremen and Supervisors," Gordon W. Hines, General Manager of the Standard Works, Surmanco, Ltd., in Sheffield, England, tells the story of a large corporation that employed a somewhat grim-looking senior-accountant-type person to sit in a glass-fronted office in view of all other staff. All employees were notified that he would check all expense accounts. A stack of expense accounts was carried in each morning and placed on this man's desk.

Although the employees didn't know it, he did absolutely nothing with them during the day. Every evening the stack was carried out to the accounting department. In little less than one month, the expense accounts showed a decrease to some 80 percent of what they had been before!

The story may be fiction, but Hines's point is true: "Whether you are actually checking the productivity of your employees is not the question. Your presence automatically increases their productivity. Too many foremen," says Gordon Hines, "prefer sitting in an office to being out on the floor."

NOTE: Apropos of the above, a general superintendent of an automobile plant pulled a fast one on his foremen and general foremen. He ordered all chairs taken out of all factory offices for a week, to keep his bosses on their feet, talking to their men down the line. "From now on, he said, "I want everyone with a supervisory job to keep circulating. We're getting too many desk men around here!"

Meet Two-Way-Vision Janus

Did you ever hear of Janus? He was an ancient Roman deity who was invoked before all other gods at the beginning of any important undertaking. Representations of him have been found on old Roman coins—a stern-visaged, bearded god with two heads on one neck facing in opposite directions. He could see in two directions at the same time, with unblinking two-way vision.

When it comes to fighting mistakes and errors on the job, every supervisor must, in effect, be a Janus. He or she has to look in two directions. One gaze has to concentrate on employees, to be sure that they're doing the job *right*—following instructions, employing approved methods, guarding against off-standard work, keeping their mind on the job to prevent careless slip-ups, and using their heads when emergency situations break into established routines.

But the other gaze has to be directed at a mirror, so that he can see himself. What is *he* doing to prevent mistakes from happening, and to minimize their effect when they do occur (as they will, every now and then, in every organization made up of human beings)?

In the long run, that "mirror look" will be the most important one of all. In your own case, for example, what are you doing to *motivate* your people to turn out their best work? Boredom and indifference are the parents of carelessness. Are *working conditions* conducive to high-level performance? Are the new workers and the slow workers getting enough *direct supervision*? Do all of your employees know exactly *what's expected* of them? Are you *consistent* as well as *insistent* in your demands for quality production—

113

i.e., do you blow your top on Wednesday over something you let get by without a peep on Monday? Or do you pass work by Mary that you wouldn't accept from Fred? Do you let pressure situations get to you to the extent of projecting your own nervousness to the department?

Think it over, Janus!

Don't Forget the Acid Test!

The following story was told some years ago to an audience of graduating business administration students by Julius Fried, founder and then president of National Shoes Inc.

National Shoes had just concluded an intensive (and expensive) training program for the managers of its hundreds of shoe stores spread over the eastern part of the country. The point of the program, conducted by an outside firm of psychologists and sales-training experts, was to instill in managers, and have them, in their own training programs at the stores, instill in their clerks, the quality of *sales resourcefulness*. The idea was to arouse customer interest in merchandise related to the initial purchase (for instance, to make companion sales of ties, socks, and handkerchiefs after selling a pair of shoes).

The training program was a huge success—that is, said Mr. Fried, sales managers, district managers, and store managers were loud in their testimonials about "a great program," "inspiring meetings," "got a lot out of them," "should make us all better managers," and so on.

However, the president decided to make a small private check of his own. Through a temporary help service he engaged some crews of "customers" who were advanced adequate funds and instructed to go into the company's stores and buy anything and everything the sales clerks tried to sell them; they were to put up no sales resistance whatsoever. Although the merchandise was, of course, to be turned in, the stores were to be given full credit for the sales, and all purchases were to remain as a regular record of sales by the individual clerks.

Result: After all the expensive training, time after time these shoppers left a store with nothing under their arms but a pair of shoes!

A parting thought on checking

Give me a system that will wave yellow flags in my face when I am heading into trouble, but wave them early enough for me to do something about it. What I never want you to do is to wave a *red* flag at me, so that whole projects and programs must come to a screeching stop because of some unforeseen holdup.

—*Major General J. B. Medaris*

PART FOUR

THE PEOPLE
EQUATION

Leadership and Motivation

A Wonderful System—But...

Virginia Tyler was supervisor of a large office operation at corporate headquarters. She had phoned the controller to say that she wanted to talk to him about the new management procedures that a firm of management consultants had installed. The controller had told her to come right up. He had a lot of respect for Virginia's ideas; if there was something in the new procedures that didn't sit well with her, the consultants would have to come up with some persuasive arguments.

"Okay, Virginia, let's have it," he said after the pleasantries of greeting were over. "What's wrong with the Smartt Associates' recommendations? I thought we had all agreed that their management-by-exception approach was just what we needed. As a matter of fact, I've been looking at our clerical-cost and related customer complaint reports, and everything looks—"

"Wonderful," Virginia cut in, finishing the sentence for him. "I don't have a complaint about the basic system itself. I see the reports too, of course. But—"

"Before we get to your reservations," said the controller, "let's recap what they've done.

"As I see our clerical system now, all of our routine documents are being processed with little or no attention required from anyone above the level of clerk. You and a lot of other managers are certainly freed of a lot of checking on matters that aren't worth your time. For your operations, you helped set the policy guides that call for your own or higher review—the review by exceptions. And with special supervisory attention now to the exceptions that

123

arise from human input errors, we've cut down on those, too. The clerical-cost figures show it."

"I know all that, Mr. Goodman," Virginia replied, "and I'm among the first to give Smartt Associates points for what they've done. But, as I said, there's still a *but.*"

"So what did I miss?" Mr. Goodman wanted to know.

"It's the review of that big class of exceptions due to human error that's creating a problem the engineers didn't take into account," explained Virginia. "We—management—are getting all the good news, in terms of lowered costs and fewer customer complaints and all the rest. But all the clerks get is the bad news."

"How so?" asked the controller.

"All the feedback to them is negative," said Virginia. "And that's what I want to change. Errors create exceptions and only exceptions get management attention. As a result, the inputting clerk gets attention only for errors. As I look at it, this is a classic example of how management systems can be efficient in a mechanical sense, but fall down when it comes to satisfying human needs."

Mr. Goodman nodded. "I see what you mean," he said. "That could lead to turnover and other problems in the long run. So what's the answer?"

"We've got to *humanize* the system," said Virginia. "My idea, for openers, is to fix up the system so that the total effect of the feedback is at least neutral, rather than totally negative. Look at this report I've developed." (She leaned over and laid a spread sheet on Mr. Goodman's desk.) "Here's a periodic error report that goes to the clerks. Besides flagging errors, this gives them a neutral target score to shoot for. And it gives supervisors a figure against which an improvement would be an occasion for praise. With this kind of report, a clerk might have to deal with an exception caused by an error, but he or she could also have an overall improvement in the error score.

"I know this will work in my operations. I suggest that we get other department heads to follow along the same lines, and—"

"I've got the idea," said Mr. Goodman. "I'm putting it down on the agenda for the others to take a crack at. See you at the regular department-head meeting this afternoon. And thanks."

How Many Leadership Hats Do You Have?

"Boy, is he *tough*! He tells you what he wants you to do, and that's it. Period. No argument. No back talk."

"He's easy to get along with, as long as you do your job. But he lets you know what's required, and helps you work out the problems, if any. And he'll listen to your own ideas, too."

"Sure, I report to him, but actually I'm my own boss. He goes by results. Lets me know what he wants, and it's up to me to produce."

Question: Which kind of "boss" are you?

Answer: All three kinds, and maybe some in-between—if you've got the normal range of people working for you. Consider the following typical "scenes from real life." The situation in all three is one where there's too much spoiled work and scrap. The general foreman has had a meeting on the subject with all supervisors and key people, but three key operations under supervisor Art Rednick are still running up poor records. The key people involved are Tom, Dick, and Harry. Scenes 1, 2, and 3 show Art talking to each one of them in turn:

Scene 1: "Tom, you're not following any of the new procedures on checking machine settings and doing self-inspection to cut down your scrap and reject record. It's worse than ever. I've gone over your job orders, and had Mike look at your machine and fixtures, as you know. Now here's what I want you to do, starting now. . . . And believe me, that scrap record on this month's report is gonna come down, or I'm *really* gonna sound off!"

125

Scene 2: "Dick, I notice that your scrap and reject record isn't hitting the mark yet, despite everything we said we'd do. I've got all of your recent job orders and scrap and reject records in my office. After lunch, stop in and let's review the problem. Maybe you've got some ideas on what we can do that we're not doing now. Joe will be there, from Quality Control, to double-check on their procedure."

Scene 3: "Harry, I know you've been tied up on that widget run. But look at your last month's scrap report. Do whatever's necessary, will you? We'll analyze the variance report again when it comes up on the 10th. Meantime, if you've got any problems, let me know."

In the above scenes, the same supervisor has been exercising three kinds of leadership, which the psychologists like to identify by some impressive-sounding names: the first, the "Boy-is-he-tough!" kind, they call "authoritarian," or "autocratic." The second, the "lets-you-know-what's-required-and-helps-you-work-out-the-problem" kind, they call "democratic," or "participative." And the third, the "you're-actually-your-own-boss" kind, which the supervisor can apply if he's fortunate enough to have the right calibre people on the job, they call "delegative leadership."

The terms themselves, and the examples, should make the meanings clear. But the big lesson for us in Art's three handlings of the same problem is that they illustrate three kinds of *leadership*, not three kinds of *leaders*—and that's something that the books and lectures on the subjects don't always make clear. You can't decide to be an "authoritarian" leader, or a "democratic" leader, or a "delegative" leader. Depending on circumstances, you have to be all three, and more.

To be a good leader, a supervisor must have made it his business to learn about people: why they act the way they do, what they will respond to, how to put them at ease, how to direct and criticize without antagonizing, how to make a new employee a productive member of his working group. He has to *know his own people.* Who are the self-starters, the self-supervisors? Who can handle responsibility? Who are the stubborn ones? Who has to be told in no uncertain terms what to do, or else? Who needs coaching and special treatment?

In short, a good supervisor has to have at least three "leadership hats," and to know when to wear each one!

Are You in This Scene?

Could the following scenario, with minor changes, have been taken from your department?

A consultant in a plant engages in conversation with the foreman in a marking department. He has been watching a group of women on the line, and asks, "Does a marker ever know the results of her work?"

"Well, no . . . not exactly. She just does it, and it's usually OK."

"What standards have you set for 'OK' or better work?"

"It has to be done right and fast enough to keep up."

"I see. And do employees know how they stand?"

"Well, if they don't hear from me, they know it's all right."

Are You Building a Cathedral?

A man walking along a country road, so the story goes, paused to watch some workmen on what appeared to be the early stages of a considerable construction project. He asked one of them what the project was that he was working on.

"I'm shaping these stones," was the reply, "so they will fit perfectly when I lay them one on top of the other."

A few moments later, the passerby put the same question to a second workman nearby, who appeared to be doing the same kind of work. This man looked up and nodded to a stretch of his completed work.

"As you can see," he said, "I'm building a wall," and returned his attention to trimming a stone carefully and testing its fit.

The stranger then came to a third man, again to all appearances engaged in the same occupation as his two fellows. Curious to hear what his response would be, he asked him also what it was that he was working on.

The man stood up proudly, and said, *"I'm building a cathedral!"*

A woman in a factory was gluing little pieces of wood on to lever arms. A consultant who was making a study in the plant asked her what her job was. "Oh," she said, *"I build pianos!"*

The foreman of a steel shop in an automobile plant was having troubles about complaints from other departments receiving his output. When he looked into the problem, he discovered that many of the men working on the shaping of large metal sheets didn't know how these were being made into automobile bodies in the very next department!

People laying bricks with blinkers on their eyes won't raise their eyes to the skies.

Ted Takes a Second Look

Ted Robertson's company had cooperated with the hard-core employment program of the National Alliance of Businessmen, and had recruited a sizeable number of people from disadvantaged areas, as well as accepting trainees furnished under the Manpower Training and Development Act. But this was by no means sheer charity; all supervisors were expected to get the new workers up to acceptable production levels as soon as possible, even though normal education, skill, and health requirements for entry-level jobs had been greatly relaxed.

But the supervisors were having a lot of headaches in the process. They didn't particularly mind the problems of extra training and close supervision involved; what really teed them off were problems of routine discipline and "tending to business." Particularly troublesome was the matter of attendance and lateness, and this had been the subject of some heated discussion at the supervisors' meeting just concluded.

"The whole program's for the birds," Al Carter, one of Ted's fellow supervisors, had proclaimed. "You can't do anything with these people. They don't know the meaning of work and discipline—and never will."

There had been pretty general agreement. "If they don't care enough to show up for the job—every day and *on time*—all our bother and extra effort are wasted. I wish we'd never been caught up in this do-gooder program," Herb Dean had said. And Jack Bauman had chimed in with, "I'm just waiting for the standard probation period to be over before getting rid of most of my problem cases."

But Ted wasn't satisfied. There had been more heat and light at that meeting, and he personally wasn't ready to write off the program. Some of the people with whom he had been having attendance problems were actually pretty good manpower material. He decided to get some facts.

What he found out was quite illuminating. And when he took the results up with Personnel, they did some more detailed investigation and immediately inaugurated some corrective measures. It added up as follows:

- He found that one of his trainees was chronically late because he couldn't read the route signs on city buses. This particular case was a language problem, and Personnel found some parallel situations caused by some unexpected reading deficiencies.

  Corrective measure: Special instruction sessions on how to get to the job were held, and some employees who spoke only broken English were given mimeographed cards which they could show to bus drivers or dispatchers, or to friendly strangers, if they were confused or lost.

- Quite a number of the new workers were from areas that were miserably served by available public transportation. Long walks to bus stops were involved, transfers had to be made, and buses were few and far between.

  Corrective measure: Car pools were arranged with some of the regular workers, who volunteered to go out of their way for pickups (mileage reimbursement was authorized). The company management persuaded the bus company to do some rerouting. And for one locality, Personnel actually arranged for chartered bus service in the morning and at the end of the day.

- A number of the women had problems with small children, and absenteeism and lateness were caused either by childhood illnesses, or by no-shows on the part of babysitters. *Corrective measure*: The employees were given instructions on how to contact the city's visiting nurse service, and the company's own program of visiting nurses was stepped up. With the aid of one of the city agencies (after the problem was taken up with other companies that had unearthed similar difficulties), day nurseries were established in certain localities. Also, special working hours were established in certain hardship cases.

- In looking into a matter of chronic absenteeism on the part of one employee who had terrific, recurring toothaches, Ted was horrified to discover that people from poverty backgrounds may never visit a dentist in their whole lives. Following up on this, the personnel department arranged for special examinations, and discovered that many of the new employees had few or even no sound teeth, and had other minor but nagging medical problems.

  Corrective measure: The new employees were urged to take advantage of a stepped-up medical counselling program, involving company-financed referrals to outside doctors in special cases.

"You triggered some good results on that lateness problem, Ted," remarked the plant manager a couple of supervisory meetings later. Ted felt good. The Old Man was a tough taskmaster and didn't hand out compliments lightly.

The Big Little Things

"Joe," said the company president to the plant personnel manager, "you'd think that after that husky wage increase and big fringe benefits package we settled for, people would seem a little more chipper and cheerful around here. How come I sense so much chip-on-the-shoulder attitude when I try to pass a few words with people in the plant?"

Joe decided to do a little birddogging. Here is what he found:

Lucy: Ever since the cold weather set in, I asked Fred [her foreman] to fix the draft at this window. I've had a stiff neck since last October. Yes, I like the wage increase—but I sure wish Fred would get this window fixed!

Tom: They moved us over to this far end of the building, and the noon lunchwagon doesn't come anywhere near us. We've griped about it to the boss for six weeks, but nothing is ever done about it.

Dick: See how I have to reach for these parts I'm screwing together? I made a suggestion to Frank [*his foreman*] a month ago about a simple rack that would save that extra motion, speed up my work, and keep me from stooping. He told me he'd think it over. Frank sure must think slow! I haven't heard a word from him since.

Harry: The way the foreman assigns overtime around here has always been a pain in the neck. We got together, and all agreed on a common-sense rotation plan. They made me spokesman, and I brought it up with him. All I got was a quick brush-off—no explanation, no discussion, just a brush-off. The raise is fine, but why don't they treat us like human beings?

Myrna: The fringe benefits are fine, but the john in the women's washroom is stuck again. It was stuck last week, too. I'll trade some of the fringe benefits for some good plumbing work!

Qualities You Don't Think You Have

Supervisor Carl Flack was surprised to find on his monthly progress report that he was considered argumentative by employees and other supervisors. He had never considered himself argumentative, and asked to discuss his rating with the department head. He suggested that his report had probably been mixed up with somebody else's.

"But I don't get mad at people much," he protested, when told that the report was indeed his own. "How can they accuse me of arguing when I'm not mad?"

"Well, Carl," the boss answered him, "I wondered about that, too, and began to watch you. I observed that when one of your people, or another supervisor, brought up a point about the job, you immediately raised your voice when answering, and you *sounded* mad. So other people think you *are* mad. That's how arguments get started. Watch yourself for a while, and I'm sure you'll lick that habit."

Carl started to answer, and his voice rose immediately. When the department head began to grin instead of arguing back, Carl had to grin, too. The boss had caught him in the act.

Join the BAD Guys

The *Wall Street Journal* recently reported some bizarre goings-on at twenty-three New York City hospitals: "Giant red footprints mysteriously appeared in hallways and elevators. Pictures of sinister, beady-eyed desperadoes suddenly began leering over portals. Walls were festooned with posters urging, 'Join the BAD Guys!'"

It turned out that the whole thing was a campaign by the hospital administrators to enlist the support of everyone in the organization, from the lowliest orderlies to the chiefs of staff, to motivate them to find ways to cut costs—in line with pressure from the federal government to slow down the surge in hospital charges.

Joining the BAD Guys meant joining everyone in saving at least a "Buck-A-Day." During an intensive four-week campaign, all workers were urged to give their bosses at least one idea on how the hospital could save a dollar a day throughout the year.

"Little cost-cutting measures can amount to considerable sums," said Larry Choby, an administrator at New York's Lenox Hill Hospital. "The average employee doesn't always know whom to go to with ideas, or perhaps he or she doesn't always feel management is responsive. But BAD got people interested."

BAD was the creation of Industrial Motivation, Inc. Although originally designed for industrial companies, it caught on with hospitals several years ago, and has been used by about 200 of them nationally. The consulting firm promises to refund its charges if the savings don't at least equal them. So far, no refunds to hospitals have had to be made.

Prime targets were outlets for energy, food, general housekeeping, and paperwork. For example, to save energy, Lenox Hill assigned an employee to turn off twenty radiology machines each evening, and the electric bill was reduced by a $7,500 annual rate. At New York's Cabrini Hospital, an employee suggested that half the elevators be shut down after 9 P.M. And St. Anthony Hospital Medical Center in Rockford, Illinois, began saving $1,000 annually on natural gas when employees followed the procedure of putting a stainless steel box in the equipment sterilizer when small loads were cleaned so that the entire sterilizer didn't have to be used.

Abraham Lincoln Memorial Hospital, in Lincoln, Illinois, followed an employee's suggestion to use a coffee extender that doubled the cups brewed per pound of coffee, saving $3,000 a year. Another hospital found it was throwing out about $1,000 worth of milk a year before it instituted a rule under which patients had to ask for milk instead of automatically receiving it on meal trays.

York Hospital, in York, Pennsylvania, saved $1,500 a year by discontinuing use of salt, pepper, and sugar packets marked with its name, and another $12,000 a year by switching to rolls of paper towels from single sheets in bathrooms. Mercy Hospital in Miami saved $12,000 a year by switching to powder cleaners instead of aerosols.

Laundry and linens are another good BAD target. Mercy saved $18,200 a year by using disposable pillows. Brooklyn Hospital planned to eliminate absorbent half-sheets on top of mattress sheets; to prevent wet mattresses, it would use disposable plastic sheets and save $5,000 in laundering.

Paperwork costs were also attacked. A Montefiore Hospital employee in New York showed how $600 in postage could be saved each year by handing out W-2 tax forms rather than mailing them. Another hospital decided to send out certain routine reports to doctors monthly instead of weekly, since the doctors usually see the data anyway on the patients' charts before they receive the mailings.

Of course, the tough test in any motivational effort such as BAD is how costs are held down on a continuing basis, over the long pull. But an immediate plus is that employee morale is up, and everyone is cost conscious. And at the very least, the savings initially achieved are "in the bag."

The Case of the White Steering Wheels

A customer service company, in ordering a new fleet of trucks, specified pure white steering wheels.

"How come?" the truck salesman asked the purchasing vice president.

"Just a bit of psychology," was the reply. "You know that J. B. [the president of the firm] is a stickler for making good impressions on customers. Those white steering wheels will encourage the drivers to keep their hands clean."

Why the Big Bridge Fell

At 11:50 A.M. on October 15, 1970, a 393 1/4-foot span of the magnificent, new West Gate Bridge in Melbourne, Australia—then still under construction—suddenly collapsed upon the workers' shacks and construction facilities along the Yarra River below. It was one of the world's worst bridge-building disasters. As a newspaper account described it:

> Span 10/11 had buckled downward near the middle. As a 19-ton crane, and oil tank, and huts on the docking tumbled like ninepins toward the center of the buckle, the falling girders slammed into Pier 11. With a thundrous rumble, the 160-foot pier disintegrated and, with the span itself, collapsed into the bank and into the river in a shower of mud, water, and rubble. As torn electrical cables ignited ruptured oil tanks, huts caught fire and bottles of oxyacetylene gas began exploding.

Of the sixty-five men on the site, thirty-five died. Additionally, there were millions of dollars of damage, and redesign and reengineering costs, as well as penalties for delays in completion, and engineering reputations were ruined.

Designed by a world-famous engineering firm, with steelwork and construction by equally renowned engineers and contractors, the West Gate Bridge was supposedly destined to be one of the wonders of the world. What went wrong?

The Royal Commission which investigated the disaster made the following flat pronouncement: "Mistakes, miscalculations, errors of judgement, and sheer inefficiency. Error begat error." Further it said, "The Authority itself [the Lower Yarra Crossing

139

Authority, which would own and operate the bridge], the designers, the contractors, even the labor engaged in the work, must all take some part of the blame."

Reports, pieced together later by the press, confirm the conviction that the engineering fault that developed (the span could not be properly joined up because of an inexplicable departure in actual measurements from what had been meticulously calculated and blueprinted) was primarily due to *poor leadership on the job*.

At first, morale and enthusiasm among the thousand or so men and women on the job were high. But as time passed, one thing after another went wrong and this spirit evaporated. There were strikes and stop-work meetings by the workers. Because of this, and poor supervision (attested to in the resultant investigation), construction was seven months behind schedule by the end of 1969, and in a desperate move, a change in steel contractors was made. Friction, however, continued.

Communications with the engineering headquarters in London seemed to have broken down. Labor disputes, often for the most trivial reasons, continued to slow up the work. (For example, when a messenger girl returned with a serving of fish and chips instead of the hamburger requested by one of the men, a whole crew stopped work until the correct order was brought in.) A section engineer testified that "men would often just take a day off simply because they felt like a holiday."

Investigation into and rechecking of structural theory and design were continuing at the time of the above reports, so that one could not lay *all* blame on derelictions of on-site leadership and employee morale. But there was preponderant evidence that these human-relations factors would remain the key to this particular tragedy.

Perpetual Motion

The late Aaron Scheinfeld, founder and chairman of the international temporary-help corporation, Manpower Inc., often talked about the "people problems" of running any kind of organization. "Perhaps what it all adds up to," he said, "is a restatement of the proposition that in addition to all the advanced management techniques provided by the experts, we should not lose sight of the day-by-day currency of human relationships—the small change of productive cooperative endeavor, in addition to the large-denomination bills of profound psychological insights."

How often, he asked, do we say "Thank You!"? We may have a subordinate whose performance is uneven; for some periods his record is very good, and for others there is a slump. Obviously, if continued and pronounced, this may be a sign of some serious personal difficulty. But have we tried the simple device of going out of our way to write him a note of commendation on one of his good weeks or months, or to congratulate him for some outstanding handling of a single assignment?

As a case in point, Mr. Scheinfeld cited a plant where one of the foremen had copies made of the daily log which he, along with other foremen, had to turn in, listing various kinds of operating information and some of the production figures for his shift.

When one of the hourly employees had a good day, this foreman would circle his name and good record, and add a few comments like, "Nice job, Joe," or "Another good day, Pete. Keep it up!" He would then see that the copy was delivered to the employee. "That," said Mr. Scheinfeld, "is one way of management's saying 'Thank you.' What more companies need is a positive 'people program'—and ongoing activity, not merely an acceptance of a philosophy. The energy such an activity will create is limitless. It is the only kind of perpetual motion that works!"

If Only We Could "Tell More Flowers"

Harry Drake was driving Estralita home—the new woman, recently arrived from Guatemala, who from now on was to come once a week to help his wife with the housework until the new baby came. She had been recommended by Mrs. Goodwin, a friend of Lucille's, and this was her first day.

Estralita was a happy kind of person, and in her not-too-good English she was telling Harry how much she had enjoyed working for Lucille.

"Mrs. Goodween tell me much about Mrs. Drake," she said. "She tell me many flowers about her."

It took a couple of seconds for that to sink in, and then Harry knew what she was driving at. Mrs. Goodwin had "told her many flowers" about Lucille—that is, she had said many nice things about her.

"Tell many flowers about someone," he mused. The words had a nice sound and perfume to them—and a nice *feel*. "If only we all could remember to tell more flowers about people," he thought, "it would probably make all of our jobs a lot easier!"

A parting thought on motivation

I hear a lot of people say pro players get paid and that's why they should do well. Well, I'll tell you something: When it's fourth and one in the fourth quarter and that monkey is on my big round-eared tackle's back and he's got a little blood up his nose and he's hurting, it doesn't make any difference whether you pay him $1,000 or $5,000 or $50,000. If he's not self-motivated, if he doesn't believe, you can't pay him enough money to make the block. . . . It has to come from pride and character, and it's the same in high school, college, or pro.

—Chuck Knox, now coach of the Buffalo Bills, in an interview in the *Los Angeles Times*

Communicating

"Plus One and Point 13"

Al Learner, supervisor at Frobish and Company was copping a ride home with Fred Smiley, the salesman covering the eastern territory for the company. (Al's car was laid up for the day with a slight case of transmission trouble.) Fred had come in for the company's annual sales meeting and had given a talk on "Sales Power" that afternoon for the benefit of the sales trainees. He was still keyed up and was telling Al all about it.

"I hammered home on 'Plus One and Point 13,'" he said. "It's an almost surefire formula. I hope those young guys got as much out of it as I did when I heard it for the first time at *my* trainee session from old man Frobish himself."

"Plus one?" said Al. "What is it? I suppose you mean Numero Uno—yourself, in other words? But then what's number 13"

"Plus One is just the opposite," laughed Fred. "And number 13 was the last point in Mr. Frobish's sales power formula. I'm frank to admit I've long since forgotten what the eleven points in between were, but those two have always stuck in my mind and I owe all of my topnotch sales awards to them.

"Plus One means *the other fellow's self-interest*. You always start out a sales pitch by opening with some problem of *his* that your product or service is about to lick, or some way in which it will make his life easier, or help assure his success. And after you've captured his interest in that way and have put across your story, number 13 comes in—the 'Action Close'. Don't leave the matter dangling. Have an order form or maybe a request for a demonstration ready to sign. Or if it's an ad or a sales letter, close by hav-

149

---

ing a coupon for the reader to send in for an order or a trial sample or whatever. But *call for action*."

Fred let Al off at his corner. As he walked the block and a half to his house, Al had something to ponder. "Plus One" and "Action Close," he mused. "I can't win a topnotch sales award, but that formula can sure help me be a topnotch supervisor! When I talk to any of my people about a change in company policy, or a new way of doing something, or the need to improve present performance, I'm going to be careful to start with Plus One. After all, every new way of doing something has a plus for them—making work easier, or adding to their earning power, or maybe helping assure their jobs by improving the company's earnings. And Plus One also is going to be my opener in reports and presentations to management.

"Then, Point 13—Action Close—is certainly in order every time: who is to do what, when, and where. Thanks for the sales formula, Messrs. Frobish and Smiley!"

Is Your Safety Message Getting through the Filter?

A young mother was talking about a recent experience at a department store in the midst of frantic special-sale shopping. She had left her small daughter in a certain section of the toy department, admonished her to remain there while mother stepped across to Notions for a few minutes.

The store's well-modulated public address system, she said, had been talking away softly but incessantly all the time she was in the store, but just on the fringe of her awareness—a faint buzzing in her ears.

"Suddenly," she said, "loudly, clearly, I heard the speaker say, 'Mrs. W—, Mrs. W—. Come pick . . . .'"

The buzzing had suddenly come through, loud and clear, *on the special frequency of her own immediate self-interest.*

Have you checked to see if your safety message is on your employees' frequency? Most companies do a lot of publicizing about safety—through booklets, employee-paper articles, posters, and occasional contests. The danger here is that unless these safety messages get the right kind of personalized follow-through by supervisors, there is a danger that the constant repetition of the safety sermon may cause it to become a faint buzzing in the ear. The people to whom it is directed are automatically filtering it out, and like the mother in the story, only a message tuned to their self-interest frequency will get through.

To get through the filter, a supervisor has to "talk up" safety in his department, relating it to his department's work. When a safety poster is changed on the bulletin board, mention it in terms of the work of the department. If an accident occurs elsewhere in the plant (or in the plant down the street), talk about it in terms of possible similar hazards in your own operations. Check up on the way your older service employees are breaking in new people—are they including the safety factors in every task's set of "key points"?

Secure employee participation by having all of your people rotate as special "safety observers" to spot unsafe conditions or practices in the department. If an unsafe condition or practice is noticed, decide whether it might pay to stop all work then and there and have a few minutes of discussion with everyone doing related work, pointing out what was wrong, and why, and what the right way is. Don't be afraid of scare tactics: If a serious accident happened elsewhere, give all of the gory details to your people so that they see the picture in all of its painful details. If a near accident happened in your department, use the same scare tactics, stressing the grim "might have beens."

Invisible Walls

"The house-wrecker's steel ball and bulldozer will knock down and clear away any *physical* wall in the world," an industrial psychologist told a management audience. "It's the *invisible walls* surrounding people and departments that cause the trouble, and are costing all of us a lot of money."

"The invisible walls," he went on to say, "are not made of bricks and concrete, but they're just as real, and a lot more difficult to tear down."

The barriers he was talking about are the invisible walls that shut off communication and prevent Mr. A from really hearing what Mr. B has to say, and keep department C from working smoothly with department D. Unless we succeed in breaking them down, we'll have foul-ups and delays and customer ill will, despite all of the marvels of modern communications. Maybe we can't "see" them (since they're invisible), but we can learn to *recognize* them, and the mere act of recognition will lead to conscious corrective measures. For example:

1. Failure to see the overall picture. This is the wall of insularity. The manager of a particular product or a particular operation hasn't really been made to see how his activity fits into the overall objective. When there are shortages or emergencies or things in general are "tough all over," he fights tooth and nail to optimize his own particular operations, and devil take the hindmost. His idea of expediting is to bulldoze through for his own particular requirements, no matter how it unbalances a preceding or following activity.

153

Barrier breakers: disseminate information; explain company policy; give background; fill people in.

2. *Departmental myopia.* This can affect employees all the way down the line, not merely managers. Like No. 1, it's a form of insularity, but it is based not on aggressive selfishness, but on ignorance of what problems others have to contend with. *Result*: failure to make allowances, failure to cooperate, readiness to criticize.

Barrier breakers: job rotation in training courses and *experience rotation* for people who have settled in their jobs. For example, some companies have had key people from the plant spend several weeks going along with salesmen on their customer calls, and have had salesmen put in a brief stint at the plant. It works for higher executives, too. Thus Parke, Davis & Company had seventy executives spend two days in the field working with experienced salesmen. A number had never before been in the field. Less elaborate techniques are plant tours and interdepartmental meetings.

3. *Inability (unwillingness) to step into the other fellow's shoes.* The two-dollar word is lack of "empathy." Root causes are basic differences in background, ingrained prejudices, and often plain mental laziness.

Barrier breakers: education, education, education—a positive program of mind-stretching. For example, a supervisor was asked to visit the homes of ghetto employees to find a cause for chronic absenteeism other than the "laziness" which he had claimed was the reason. He found that he had not had the slightest conception of how many of the disadvantaged element of the city lived, and how wide the cultural gap was. Where joblessness was a way of life, and being on welfare a normal mode of economic existence, there was not the same concept of time and punctuality taken for granted with people conditioned to working disciplines and the imperatives of eight-to-five time frames. The first family he visited had never owned an alarm clock! One visit didn't cure the particular worker's problem, but it gave the supervisor a new understanding and a more patient approach in coaching and indoctrination.

4. *A don't-listen climate.* This is the failure by managers (often stimulated by top management's attitude) to realize that communication is a two-way operation; it must flow up as well as down. If suggestions are ignored or definitely not encouraged, if

good ideas aren't given credit, and if complaint and grievance procedures are practically nonexistent, management's "don't-listen" attitude is soon matched by employee "what's-the-use?" attitudes. *Result:* when emergency situations come up that require full employee cooperation, management wonders why it doesn't seem able to get its story across.

Barrier breakers: education, education, education—directed to managers instead of to workers. (A large body of literature on the subject is available, and many consultants and communications specialists stand ready to help.) And a positive program of *listening!*

How Bill Jergens "Deautomated" the Rumor Mill

Rumors were flying thick and fast in the company where Bill Jergens was a supervisor. At the bowling game the night before, one of his men said he had it first hand from somebody over in Accounting that the computer system the company was putting in would cause a wholesale layoff in the clerical staff. In the washroom that morning, he overheard old doleful Joe sounding off about how the new automatic line with its complicated tape controls would "call for a whole new breed of operators," and that people like himself and a lot of others would be out on the street. Right after lunch even steady old Hank Hardfast said he had heard something over the transom at Production Control that indicated the computer system was going to be tied into factory operations with a whole new scheme of tight control that would cut into individual incentive earnings.

So Bill Jergens realized it was high time he got some straight facts to set against the "I heard this" and "they say that" noise cluttering up the grapevine. Here is what he found out (his own superior was surprised to learn of the stories going the rounds, and said there weren't any secrets about the new installation), and he got some of his key men together at coffee break to get his "counter-propaganda" started:

Item: The new computer was, indeed, going to be a fairly

156

large-scale installation. But there weren't going to be any whole-sale office layoffs. There would be a big net saving in personnel, but, believe it or not, turnover in those routine clerical jobs was close to 50 percent a year, and normal attrition rates would more than take care of the force reduction.

Item: The new automated equipment for the plant would in-deed call for some adjustments in job content and skill re-quirements. But the company had been making detailed analyses of existing worker skills as against the demands of the planned technological changes, and the conclusion of the consultants who had been studying the situation was that the new skill requirements were well within the learning capacity of the majority of the regular workforce. Personnel was already putting together ap-titude tests and training programs to which all would be eligible, and which would be conducted on company time.

Item: Yes, the computer was going to reach into the plant. But what was involved were some strategically located input stations, on which a worker would, with a prepunched card, flash instant updating information to the central computer whenever he com-pleted a job.

Result: Better inventory and production-control records, fewer mistakes, less pencil work, better planning, and in all probability *increased* individual incentive earnings.

Mr. Negative, Meet Mr. Positive!

Paul's supervisor, Joe Negative, was really teed off!

"For crying out loud, Paul, you know better than that! When I turned that green kid over to you to get started on the job, I expected you to keep an eye on him and go through the 'showing-them-the-ropes' procedure we worked out for getting new people started. You're an old hand around here, and I shouldn't have had to remind you. Now I've got that spoilage record to explain to the boss."

Paul didn't have much of an answer to that chewing out. He knew he was in the wrong, and he kicked himself mentally the rest of the morning. Sure he should have handled that business about the new kid better. Only, he had been in the middle of that rush job. He wondered if any of the other guys had heard the dressing down. And here he thought he was in line for that assistant supervisor opening. Guess he could kiss that goodbye! And how could he concentrate on this blasted parts list now? Oops!—that column was added up wrong. How many others had he slipped up on while his mind was wandering? Better do those others over. . . .

In another department, almost the same scenario had been taking place, but the script was different:

Harry's supervisor, Fred Positive, was talking to him about that blooper with the new kid.

"Look, Harry," said the boss. "You're one of our best men —that's why I turned the kid over to you. What went wrong, anyway? Remember our 'showing-them-the-ropes' procedure?"

"I guess I shoulda told you about that rush job," said Harry. "I thought you knew—and I didn't know the kid was a real greenhorn. I'm sure sorry about that spoiled work. What do you want me to do?"

"I should have checked with you about your workload, I guess," answered Fred. "My fault there. But Harry, you still had a responsibility. So the next time a situation like this comes up, remember what happened on this one. Neither of us will take anything for granted—about your workload and about how much any new employee knows. Meanwhile, I'll handle that spoiled-work report without bruising anyone."

Harry got the message and told himself he'd be darn sure he wouldn't make the same mistake again. He was sure glad Fred would be able to handle that report with the chief. "Let's see now—I can easily finish that rush job before the noon whistle."

George Baxter Learns
a Lesson
(The Hard Way)

George Baxter was a young assistant department head in the budget department. He was a bright fellow with a head for figures, and so was given a special assignment to devote all of his time "on loan" to the vice president of Manufacturing on a project that concerned expanding the company's manufacturing facilities. Three alternatives were under serious investigation: whether to modernize and expand the existing plant; whether to close down the existing plant and build an entirely new plant in a more central location to markets; or whether to modernize (but not expand) the existing plant and build a smaller supplementary plant.

Needless to say, in this early stage the project was highly confidential.

George was full of enthusiasm about the assignment. Getting together the pertinent figures, analyzing them, and drawing up comparisons for top-level analysis were right down his alley. And, of course, he was gratified at having been singled out for the job. He got a thrill out of being invited to attend meetings with important company executives and going along with the vice president to luncheon meetings with transportation representatives, heads of community industrial committees, architects, engineers, and others. All of this gave him a pleasant feeling of importance.

One evening he went to a reunion dinner of his old high school

160

graduating class. He was delighted to run into good old Bill Channing, whom he hadn't seen for some time. They sat in a corner for predinner drinks and compared notes about what they had been doing.

Bill, it turned out, had been doing all right. He was working in the investment department of a big insurance company, and had been on some interesting trips—one of them even to Europe!—as part of a team evaluating large-scale building projects that his firm was financing.

George was glad that he could match Bill's success story with some accounts of his own assignment on the company's new plant project. Why, speaking of financing, just the other day he had been at lunch with the vice president of a Boston financing firm discussing the possibilities in a lease-purchase arrangement for well over a million dollars. (We can forgive George for neglecting to mention that he had come along with the manufacturing vice president and treasurer, in case some details of his figures had to be discussed. He carried the treasurer's briefcase.)

The next morning George's phone rang. The treasurer wanted to see him right away. "Probably about that depreciation rundown," thought George. "Boy, what would they do without me around here?" He gathered together his binder on depreciation and went to the treasurer's office.

"Sit down, George," said the treasurer, and nodded to his secretary, who immediately left the room. Somehow or other, George detected a distinct chill in the air.

"What's this I hear about your telling somebody over at Metropolis Insurance that we are planning to finance our new plant with Second Boston Corporation?" he asked.

Metropolis Insurance??? *Holy smoke!*—that was Bill Channing's company! What was going on here? Then (being quick at figures), he put two and two together... He remembered swapping success stories with Bill the night before. But what did that have to do with the treasurer?

The treasurer was leaning back in his chair, leveling a cold look at George and waiting for an answer.

"Ub dub . . . ," began George.

"I got a phone call this morning, bright and early, from Harold Farnsworth, Metropolis' Finance vice president," said the treasurer, helpfully. "You may not know it, but we've been doing business with them for years. Right now we have three million dollars of financing through them. Harold wanted to know how come we were dickering with somebody else about a new plant project. He said he got it from one of his assistants, and the assistant got it from one of *my* assistants."

George decided to come clean. He told the treasurer about the class reunion and how he had been talking with Bill and how one thing had led to another.

Luckily for George, the treasurer was a nice guy. He had respect for George's demonstrated abilities, he recognized that George was still young in the business world, but most of all he realized that George would profit by this mistake.

"Look, George," he said, softening a bit. "I know how these things go. Your friend was probably implying that he was running Harold Farnsworth's operation, and you probably had to come back with some of your own activities.

"But let this be a lesson to you. The financial community thrives on gossip and rumors. Why do you think the stock market goes up and down all day long. Never, *never* discuss financial matters (or any other confidential company business) outside of the company. The walls have ears—and I understand that in some bars there are even electronic pick-up devices in dry martini olives. I can understand your making this kind of mistake—*once.*" And he nodded dismissal, buzzing for his secretary to come back into the room.

George left in a hurry, without his usual wise cracking with the secretary. But he did remember one thing—and he never forgot it. It was that last word the treasurer had said:

"*Once.*"

No Bouquet for Frank

The hard-boiled vice president for manufacturing was giving the plant manager a hard time. He had just tossed a report on his desk, grimacing sourly as he did so.

"Frank Mudd will never be able to manage that project in Building A," he growled. "He seems to have missed—or at least obscured—the main factors in the problem."

"But Frank's one of our best men," protested the plant manager. "He's got the right technical background for the job, and he's a seasoned man. I admit his report makes for heavy reading in spots, and it's not well organized. But I know Frank knows his stuff."

"Well, if he does, it certainly doesn't come through in this," the vice president shot back, picking up the report again. "Look, he takes four pages in a rambling and repetitive discussion of the background of the project—which he should have known I already know—and when he finally gets to the nitty gritty of what should be done, he gets lost in a welter of technical jargon and detail, instead of saying clearly what should be done and when and why. I want to know what time it is, and he insists on telling me how the watch works!

"By the way, didn't you go over this report with him?"

"Well, er, yes," the plant manager answered. "As I said, it's a bit heavy going. But of course, I know the situation over in Building A. And I know Frank. I know what he can do."

"*You* may know, but *I* don't," snapped the vice president. "Now I'll tell you what I'm going to do. I'm just going to table this whole project for a week. And by that time I expect Frank to come up with a report that makes more sense than this one." He handed the sheaf of papers back to the manager. After a slight pause, he added meaningfully, "And a little editing on your part won't hurt, either."

Rx for Written Reports

For written reports, you will save yourself and the recipients a lot of time by remembering a few simple rules: a good report should have precise statements as to (1) problem or objective of the study or project reported upon; (2) data which were found to have an important bearing on the problem, and the methods used in collecting the data; and (3) conclusions, including action taken or recommended.

The outlining of major and minor points ahead of time is most important. Experience shows that the greatest difficulty of managers who rebel at report writing and unwelcome paperwork, and who turn in unsatisfactory reports, is that they have not developed the skill of "categorization"—the setting down of points in orderly fashion (I, I–A, A–1, 1–a, and so on) to provide a clear sequence. Without such prethinking, they usually fail to give equal prominence and space to points of comparable weight.

Consulting engineering firms have developed methods of report writing which can profitably be followed by any manager when he has to prepare a report for management. For example, one industrial engineering firm developed the following effective presentation pattern:

1. *Introduction*. This is a very brief statement of the objective of the study, benefits to be derived, etc.
2. *Conclusions*. These are listed in succinct paragraphs, numbered and sequenced as 1, 1–a, 1–b, 2, 3, etc.
3. *Recommendations*. These again are succinct paragraphs, listed in the same style.
4. *Discussion of Conclusions*. This is in the form of extended paragraphs under subheads numbered in the same way as the conclusions. Some summary tables are included here, but the main tables, supporting data, charts, and the like, are simply referred to here and placed in the appendix.

5. *Discussion of Recommendations.* Here extended remarks are given, as in (4) above, under subheads numbered in the same manner as the recommendations.
6. *Summary.* This is a brief restatement of the basic findings, highlighting recommended action.
7. *Appendix.* Supporting data information, as indicated above, are put here.

Do You Think by the Inch and Write by the Yard?

Few things rob letters and memo writing of strength more than wordiness, says Everett O. Alldredge, of the National Archives and Records Service. Words are like money, he points out in the *Handbook of Modern Office Management and Administrative Services*. Here are examples he gives of how expressions in some government memos could easily be deflated:

> ~~You are advised that~~ the schedule should be sent directly to this office as soon as possible.
>
> A copy is attached ~~hereto for your information and guidance~~.
>
> ~~It will be observed that~~ all messages emanating from the Washington office. . . .
>
> ~~Your attention is directed to~~ section 7 ~~which~~ says. . . .
>
> This will enable the states to get started ~~sooner than if they waited until some later date~~.
>
> The study is nearly completed ~~at the present time~~.

There is an old saying, says Alldredge: "He who thinks by the inch and writes by the yard should be kicked by the foot."

"So What?"

The president of a company told the following story during the course of a luncheon conversation:

"Last week I gave a young manager in one of our departments a proposed training program to assess. He completed the assignment and wrote me a detailed, two-and-a-half-page, single-spaced memo outlining his thoughts. After wading through the copy, I scrawled 'So what?' across the face of the memo and shunted it right back to him.

"The next day I received a four-sentence summation and action recommendation from him that told me everything I wanted to know."

Are You Guilty of 'Gunnysacking"?

Don't "gunnysack," say Paul Preston and Brian L. Hawkins, writing on appraisal and communication in the Industrial Management Society's journal, *Industrial Management*. Here is what they mean:

A manager may have an occasion to give some negative feedback to an employee. His idea is to correct one or two things in the employee's behavior, yet often these objectives get lost once the discussion is started.

Have you ever been in an argument, and when it began to get tough, someone threw in the phrase, "*Well, not only that, but . . .*"? Saving up things that annoy us can get us into trouble. When the battle starts to get really rough, we start digging out all the ammunition we can find. All those little things that have been under our skin finally have a way to get out.

All of us have been guilty of this kind of argument. As a manager you come into the session with one or two things you want to straighten out. When the employee puts up a fight, or gets defensive about some of these things, you may feel backed against a wall, and strike out with whatever is at hand. We've saved all those little gripes and put them in our gunnysack, to have them handy for the right time.

Gunnysacking detracts from efforts to correct real problems. The subordinate can now justify his or her behavior, because obviously you're just nit-picking. You dilute your message to the

168

employee if you add too many additional issues. A better strategy is to confront those minor issues as they arise. If they aren't important enough to bring up as they occur, forget about them. Don't put them in a gunnysack and then have them get in your way when something really important arises.

"Cold under the Collar" Communications

General manager J. B. Headman had what he considered a top-notch team of supervisors in his rather large department. They knew their stuff, and had developed good working teams under them, were vigilant as to costs (he had certainly drilled *that* into them!), and in general reflected favorably on his, Headman's, ability to pick good people and develop them.

But there was one difficulty: the men, and two women, were certainly gung ho in staying on the ball to get the work out, on time, of top quality and at the lowest possible cost, but these benefits didn't come for free. Their cost consciousness and push for results, and the individual drive and energy and personal ambition for which he had picked each one of them in the first place, had created serious problems of interdepartmental touchiness, poor communications, and heated charges and countercharges when one unit's work was held up because of some alleged shortcoming in another unit. And when one of those critical incidents arose that are bound to occur in every large organization, an attempt to get at the bottom of things was more likely to end up in blame-fixing and even name-calling instead of a group effort to prevent recurrence.

One day Mr. Headman happened to read a quite detailed account of a highly successful program called "Couple Communication" that had been going on for a number of years at a local university. It was designed for married or engaged couples who found that they were having increasingly serious problems of bickering and fault-finding and inability to find give-and-take solutions to issues that were beginning to divide them.

The technique was simply to get small groups of couples like that together, and get individual couples to talk out problems before the rest of the group, all of whom were complete strangers in the beginning. The emphasis was on having the talks take place in a constructive, rather than a destructive fashion. (The mere fact that there was an audience of strangers aided in this.) After a few minutes of discussion, the group was asked to comment on how the two "performers" had talked to each other, and how well they had used some common-sense principles of communication advanced in an earlier session.

Mr. Headman saw no reason why the technique had to be confined to married or about-to-be-married couples, and confirmed this by a visit to the psychologists who had created the course. With assistance from them, he set up a "Cold Collar Communications" program in his company, with the sure conviction that he had everything to gain and nothing to lose.

The procedure was simple. He commandeered a conference room (promptly dubbed the "Rumpus Room" by the participants), and explained to his managers that it would be made available to them for a series of "Communications Sessions" along the lines so successfully conducted at the university. He gave them a quick sketch of what had been working so well with the couples, and told them that they were all going to try the same technique.

The scheme was to meet once a month for a couple of months, to work out a better way to handle the kind of frictional communications problems that had been plaguing the department. Simply put, the objective was to find out how to handle hot issues without getting hot under the collar—hence the name, "Cold under the Collar Communications."

In rotation, a couple of managers would discuss, for about twenty minutes, an actual or typical situation that had created problems, in an open-ended and unstructured fashion, in front of the others, who would then dissect the communication performance.

It was stressed that the sessions would be completely off the record. Mr. Headman would not even be present, and no solutions or recommendations on any of the problems discussed were to be made. The only objective was to improve communication techniques.

One of the psychologists in the Couple Communication program had agreed to attend the first few sessions, first to give some common-sense pointers on communications (which would then be reflected in the kind of criteria the group would use in analyzing the communication performances), and second to provide an initial monitoring, after which the group would be on its own.

Here are some of the questions the "dissectors" batted around after a "performance":

- How well did the two supervisors use the communication principles presented in the previous session?
- How well did each express his feelings, thoughts, impressions, desires, and intentions?
- Did they check out their understanding of what the other had said, asking for clarification when obviously needed, rather than assuming a meaning that the other might not have intended?
- Did they steer clear of statements that were blaming, accusatory, demanding, or evasive?
- Most important, in their tone and choice of words, did they show that they respected themselves and each other, or was one putting himself or the other person down?

"I tend to talk too much without really listening," remarked one participant later. "This program made me think about what I'm trying to get across, and to *listen* and digest."

"If you see you have a problem," another remarked, "you can say, 'Wait a minute. There's a way to cope with this.' You can examine a situation before it becomes heated."

A third said, "I now have a comfortable, confident feeling about relationships with other managers. Instead of being worried about difficult situations, I know the other person and I have the skills to work out of it or around it."

The psychologist added some summing-up points: " Although we live in a highly verbal society, few of us have really learned how to talk to one another in sensitive situations. This kind of practice is no high-falutin' therapy, but it teaches techniques and provides a framework for communication that people can use the rest of their lives. It fosters good will because it takes the emphasis off of totally winning the other person over to your own point of view, and places it instead on reaching an understanding of one another's views."

Sometimes, he pointed out, the only agreement possible is that there is no acceptable ultimate solution to a problem but the decision to live with the status quo rather than one person giving in or the other suppressing his hostility.

How Much Do You Know about "What's-His-Name"?

Supervisor Vince Murphy had an embarrassing experience at an opening exercise in a seminar on "interpersonal techniques" by a visiting industrial psychologist. The entire group consisted of some forty people from various companies in the area, all with management responsibilities. For openers, the seminar leader asked them to do some intermingling, taking special care not to stay in small cliques from the same company or department.

After a few minutes of this, he rapped for attention, and said, "Now I want everyone to break up into pairs. Pick someone you didn't know before, or don't know very well, and go off by yourself for a little private conversation. I'll allow about fifteen minutes for this. Find out about each other—where you were born, where you went to school, the nickname you had when a kid, the kind of job your father had, your national origin. Each person has about seven or eight minutes. Prod each other with questions."

Vince found this experience most stimulating. His partner seemed very interested in what he had to say about himself. After using up what he thought was about half the allotted time, he asked his new friend where he came from, and just what nationality his hard-to-pronounce name represented, when the leader's whistle blew.

"Now, said the leader, "I want you to form groups of six, made up of three pairs. I'll give you three minutes to organize yourselves, and then I'll give you the next instruction." After the chairs lining the walls of the meeting room had been dragged out to form separate circles, and everyone was settled down, the leader announced the next order of business: "Start with one of the pairs, and number off, from one to six." Vince's new friend became No. 1, and he became No. 2.

"Okay," the seminar leader said. "Now, starting with No. 1, I want each of you to pretend you're your partner, and introduce yourself. This should be easy, because you've just learned all about him or her. Each of you can take five or six minutes for this."

Vince's partner started off briskly. "I'm Vince Murphy," he said. "I was born and went to school . . ."—and he went on to give an impressive six-minute story of Vince's life. Vince thought he did a pretty good job.

And then it was Vince's turn. Vince got up, and then a cold, clammy truth hit him all of a sudden. He didn't know a blessed thing about his partner, except that his nickname was "Nicky," because his long last name was Kikkikorovich or something like that. Gee, *he didn't even know his name!* What should he say? What *could* he say?

Vince gulped, hesitated, and then did what he had to do. "My name is Nicky," he said, and he leaned over to peer at his friend's name tag—"that's short for Ivan Nikrokovitch . . . but now I'm embarrassed. I don't know anything more about myself. A little while back, when I was Vince Murphy, I obviously did all of the talking. I gave Nicky the story of my life, but I didn't find out anything about Ivan Nikrokovitch, except that his nickname is Nicky, and that his family is from Lithuania."

Ivan interrupted him. "Vince, I think you just gave me that nickname. When I was a kid, everyone called me Vanny, and my family came from the Ukraine."

There was general laughter, and Vince threw himself on the mercy of the court. "Look," he said, "I learned a lot out of this. It's been a real lesson in listening. Even if nothing else happens here, this was worth the price of admission."

NOTE: Professor J. M. Jackson of the University of Kansas has described an experiment conducted among the executives of a large organization. They were asked to indicate on a checklist how much time they spent with one another, and the subject of their interaction.

In one-third of the answers, they were in disagreement about the subject of their discussions. For example, a personnel manager reported that he had been discussing personnel matters with a production man. The production man, however, said that they had been discussing questions of production. Where the executives differed, each assumed that the problem with which he was personally most concerned was what they had really been talking about; the impressions their communications had made upon them had been shaped by their own goals and motives.

Why Bob Anderson Missed Bowling Night

It was bowling night. Frank Barker, supervisor of the shipping department, was going over the roster with Jim Newcomb of Personnel who was handling the paperwork for the tournament.

"How come this line is drawn through Bob Anderson's name?" Frank wanted to know.

"Bob won't be here tonight," said the personnel man. "He's at the high school."

"What's he doing there?" asked Frank. "Bob graduated with me. What's he doing in high school now?"

"He's taking a course in conversational Spanish," said Jim.

"For crying out loud, what's he wanna do that for? Last I knew, his assembly department still gets its shop orders in English."

"Maybe so," said Jim. "But did you notice how many Spanish-speaking people we've got in the plant now? Especially since we agreed to take on a certain percentage of the so-called 'hard-core' unemployed for special training. Many of them come from that Puerto Rican section across town. Bob drew quite a lot of them for his department."

"But those people speak English. Maybe not the best, but enough to be understood," countered Frank.

"Yes, but Bob was talking to me about his department the other day. He said he wants to be able to speak *their* language. He had some Spanish in his high school days, but now he wants to brush up. Said he went to that Puerto Rican Day picnic the other day on one of his people's invitation, and wished he'd done his brushing up earlier. He wants to be able to say more than *buenos dias* and *buenos noches*, and I must say, it makes a lot of sense. Those newcomers in his department appreciate the effort he's making, the interest he's shown in them as *people*. So I guess you'll have to do without Bob tonight, but it's all for a good cause."

"Well, it may not be a great loss for the team," said Jim. "Bob never was a candidate for the world's best bowler. But I do know he's making more points at high school tonight than the rest of us are making here."

Answering the "Unanswerable"

The plant manager had called the weekly supervisors' meeting a half-hour earlier than usual. The supervisors knew something special was afoot as soon as they filed into the conference room and saw Mr. Landers, the Manufacturing v.p. from the home office, at the head of the table with Bart Williams, the plant manager.

"Fellows," said Bart, "Mr. Landers asked to sit in at the beginning of our meeting this week because of the talk about that merger that's been in the air. Mr. Landers, I believe you know all of these people except Art Hanford who's just taken over the reeling department," and he introduced the new supervisor.

"It's good to meet all of you again," said Mr. Landers. "I want to talk to you about a tough job you're all going to have for the next three weeks or so. It's *how to answer the 'unanswerable.'* I'm sure you've all heard about the possible merger of our company with Acme Windings?"

Everyone nodded. Buzzing about it was all over the place.

"You all must know," continued Mr. Landers, "that matters like this are always in a negotiating stage for an extended period—and sometimes the negotiations are delicate. A deal may be on or off, depending on all kinds of things—auditors' reports, stockholders' reactions, what's happening on the stock exchange, clearances with government agencies—I could name you dozens more.

"So if you as supervisors think you've been kept in the dark as to what's going on, maybe it's because we didn't have the answers ourselves. We'd certainly look foolish if we indicated a line of action and then had to change signals because of matters beyond our control. So the first point I want to make is that it was never our intention to spring a surprise on you at the last minute when we could have taken you into our confidence earlier.

"But now matters have reached the stage where definite statements can be made, and where you as members of management here at this plant are involved. Bart and I decided that you'd like to have the story come straight from the home office, and that's why I'm here today."

Mr. Landers then laid it on the line. The gist of what he had to say was as follows:

Yes, the merger was going through, but for legal and other reasons that he didn't think it necessary to take the time at this meeting to go into, the official announcement couldn't be made for another three weeks. But because the supervisors at this plant would have to do some advance planning, he wanted to give them all of the background, *even though under no circumstances could they pass along any of the company decisions until the president of the company had arranged for the proper form of notification to all employees, to stockholders, and to the media.*

Yes, this plant was to be closed down, but its operations would be combined with those of the more modern Acme plant in a town seventy-five miles away. Yes, some people were going to be affected adversely, no doubt about it. But at least 60 percent of the employees here would find openings (at no loss of pay) in the combined operations if they wanted to move. Effective date of the move would be six months away.

There followed considerable discussion of the kind of planning the supervisors present would have to do about relocating their departments—problems of seniority and other matters affecting choice of personnel for possible transfer, arrangements for separations, and a host of other matters.

Obviously, all of these questions couldn't be resolved at this meeting. But Bart Williams (to whom Mr. Landers had turned over the meeting when the detailed discussions began) had left enough time for what he termed the $64 question: how to handle discussions with employees for the next three weeks, during the period when the supervisors would know what the score was but couldn't divulge it. In Mr. Landers' phrase, how to answer the "unanswerable."

"Our people aren't dummies," said Bart. "A number of them

saw Mr. Landers come in. And this meeting has been running twice as long as usual. They know we're not discussing last month's back-order situation or the repair of those pot holes in the employee parking lot.

"It's a ticklish business, but it boils down to your having to be as positive and constructive as possible without revealing any classified information. But in the answers you do give, you've got to be honest. If you're not, you're going to sow distrust which can only hurt you later on."

After further discussion, and questions-and-answers, Bart summarized the guidelines for answering the unanswerable as follows:

1. Take the initiative. Arrange for a meeting with key people as soon as possible to say what you can say.
2. On the point-blank question, "Is there going to be a merger?" you can reply that there is serious talk going on, but no final decision has been made (which is true, because decisions *won't* be final for another three weeks). Don't go so far as to indicate that as far as management's *intentions* are concerned, they are final. If anyone presses you, you can always honestly say that you are obviously in no position to talk about top management's intentions.
3. Be as positive as possible. Don't go out of your way to publicize the negative, but if the question comes up, don't sugarcoat; admit frankly that if the merger goes through, some people will be adversely affected. But also emphasize the positive: this will be a good move for the company, if it does happen, because it will strengthen our competitive position, lead to further expansion and better job opportunities.
4. Emphasize the time factor. You can state positively that such and such a date has been set when an official announcement of the outcome of negotiations and deliberations will be made.
5. Acknowledge the right of employees to ask questions, even though you can't answer all of them fully. A "you-don't-have-a-right-to-know-that" attitude builds up employee resentment. A reply to the effect that "I know you're interested, but in this case all I can tell you is . . ." will usually carry you over until the time comes when you *can* be definite.

6. Emphasize that as soon as decisions are officially reached that will affect any of your people, you will inform everyone concerned immediately.

7. Underline the point that if a decision is reached that will affect anyone adversely, you are going to do everything humanly possible to help in connection with whatever personal adjustments will have to be made.

8. Close on the note that you recognize that there are always some people who worry more about uncertainties of this sort than others, and that for personal reasons (if not for reasons of temperament) they may well have a right to. Therefore, even though you can't add more at the moment to whatever you've just said, you're always ready to meet personally and privately with anyone who wants to discuss his or her personal situation.

A parting thought on communicating

   "Communication" may be the most overworked *word* and
the most underworked *act* in all of management.

                                        —*John G. Mapes*

C

Start-ups

A Comedy of Errors

(But Not So Funny After All)

Scene: The personnel department of a large plant. The personnel office is open for the night shift. A worker walks in, obviously unhappy. He asks to see the plant personnel man on duty. The personnel man comes out, and the worker hands him his badge.

"I quit," he says flatly.

"But why?" exclaims the surprised personnel man. "You're Steve Warner. You just started this afternoon! I processed your papers and took you over to the machine shop myself, at four o'clock."

"I guess I'm just not cut out to be a machine operator," says Warner, and unfolds his sorry tale.

True, he had reported for work at four o'clock, and had been escorted by the personnel man to the department to which he had been assigned, and introduced to the foreman.

After a brief talk (very brief, because the foreman had a lot on his mind), the foreman took him over to the machine where he was to work. The foreman took a blueprint from a stack, pointed out the part where it described the piece on which Warner was to work (a couple of simple holes to be drilled), inserted a piece in the machine, and did the work on it himself.

Then he turned to Warner and said, "See how it's done?" Steve didn't want to appear stupid on his first day, so he nodded. "You'll keep getting deliveries of pieces to be drilled," the foreman explained, "and you put the finished pieces here. I'll see you later." And he left.

187

Steve looked at the blueprint, picked up a piece, and started to insert it into the drill press. But before going on with that, he thought it would be a good idea to study the blueprint. The trouble was, he hadn't had any instructions in reading blueprints, and so he only became more confused.

As for the machine, it had seemed easy when the foreman did it, but now he was so nervous he couldn't remember how to position the piece and start the operation.

Steve screwed up his courage and went to the fellow on the next machine, and asked him whether he could come over and help him get the hang of things. But the other operator was on incentive work, and refused to take the time—his earnings would go down if he did. "It's the foreman's responsibility to get you started on a job," he said. "Why don't you just wait until he comes around again?"

Steve waited nervously for the foreman to show up. But when the supper whistle blew, there still was no foreman. So he left with the others. Instead of opening his lunchbox, however, he went to the personnel department, where we met him in our opening scene.

"Let's get to the bottom of this," said the personnel man, and they both went back to look for the foreman. They found Bill, the foreman, all right, and he was quite surprised at the trouble. It turned out that Bill had understood that he was getting a man with previous experience, so he took it for granted that Steve knew all about blueprints and drill-press operation. But now he admitted that his biggest mistake had been in not at least watching, after his quickie instruction, to see how Steve would turn out the first piece.

Sequel: After supper, Steve was placed with a job instructor. He later became one of Bill's best men.

"As Is" vs. "Should Be"
(Mr. Umlaut's Disoriented Orientation)

"Many supervisors contend that they are 'too busy' to provide the step-by-step explanations of procedures that a new employee requires, particularly a new employee without previous work experience," says Virgil K. Rowland, assistant to the chairman of the board of Detroit Edison Company.* "So they turn the job over to a "seasoned" employee, and the bad habits that have already taken root in the office are perpetuated." As a result, many supervisors are blithely unaware of many differences between what *is* going on, and what *should* be going on.

As a prime example of poor employee orientation, he cites the following true case. A young man who had just been hired reported, on his first day, right on time and was eager to go to work. Mr. Umlaut (name disguised here for obvious reasons), his new supervisor, greeted him pleasantly and spent the next ten minutes repeating things the young man had already heard twice before from the personnel department. Then he said, "Now I'll turn you over to Jerry Worthman. He'll tell you what to do."

Out of earshot, Jerry told the new man that he'd be glad to help him learn his job because "very confidentially," Umlaut didn't know much about the details of the work.

* In his chapter, "Orienting the New Employee," in the *Handbook of Modern Office Management and Administrative Services*, ed. Carl Heyel (Huntington, N.Y.: Krieger, repr. 1980).

The first chore on the program was a relatively simple clerical task: checking the work of typists who were transferring information from papers of original entry to books of final entry. The checking consisted of keeping a record of the routine corrections, by means of slips filed under the names of the typists.

To the new employee this seemed like a school-teacher attitude—but who was he to question an office routine on his first day? So he dutifully made out a slip every time he found a typing error.

Before the day was over, however, he was told to change his practice. Several typists had complained to Jerry that "the new jerk" was overdoing the correction bit. So Jerry told him that if he didn't want to be unpopular he would quietly take the mistakes to the typists and have them make the necessary corrections, and then forget about writing up the correction slips. This would keep the girls from looking bad in Mr. Umlaut's eyes.

By this time, the new employee was not certain that his supervisor ever noticed anything that went on. Obviously, Mr. Umlaut had never questioned why the checkers had to go see the typists so often.

He asked Jerry what good the correction slips were anyway. "Oh, that's just one of Umlaut's old womanish stunts," Jerry replied. "None of the employees likes it, so we just fill out enough slips to make him think we're on the job, but not enough to make any of the typists look bad. You've already issued more correction slips in an hour than all the other checkers do in a day. You'll get along much better if you do things the way we do."

Right here, Rowland points out, it was evident that there was a serious gap between what the supervisor thought was happening and what was actually being done. And the new employee, more confused than ever about the ways of "big business," was being oriented *on his very first day* to circumvent management rather than to follow standard operating procedures! (The quality of Mr. Umlaut's operating procedures is, of course, a whole other story.)

Why Suzie Made Mistakes, but Mary Anne Didn't

Many otherwise good employees become panicky when things begin to go wrong, or when there's a pressure situation, or even when the boss happens to be passing by. That's when bloopers pile up. The first four imaginary electrocardiograms below could record Suzie's emotions during her first day on the job. Contrast this with the last graph, which could be one taken of Mary Anne, also on her first day. Of course, they had two different supervisors.

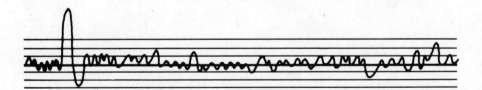

(1) Suzie's first morning. After initial uneasiness she settles down.

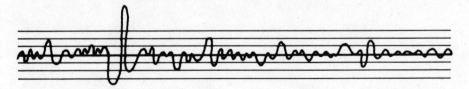

(2) Boss calls attention to mistake—not very gently.

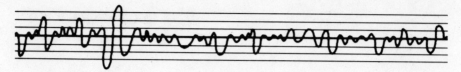

(3) Boss in neighborhood...comes close, but luckily doesn't say anything...
now he's looking at some of her work...

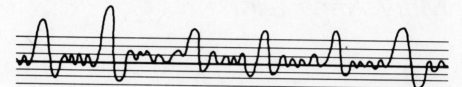

(4) Suzie wishes boss would leave the department... Who's he talking to
now??...Are they discussing her?

(5) The "electrocardiogram" of Mary Anne's first day. But she has a different supervisor entirely!

"Experienced Salespeople Need Not Apply!"

At a sales executives' association meeting, a sales manager whose company had racked up enviable increases in volume for every one of the six years since he had taken over was asked to pinpoint his secret of success.

"It's probably because I make it a point to hire only inexperienced salesmen," was the surprising reply. He was asked to explain.

"Don't get me wrong," he said, "I'm not knocking experience. But at least in the case of our specialized product, I simply don't feel x years spent in selling means the candidate for a sales job with us has a leg up on a bright young person I'll train myself. As a matter of fact, often an old pro, rather than improving his or her sales ability each year, will develop more and more bad habits. In my humble opinion, the reason behind some companies' sagging sales is that the salespeople they've hired have had too much experience for their own good.

"On the other hand, an inexperienced or greenhorn salesperson hasn't had a chance to get into a rut. He or she is more willing to try new methods to bring in sales. He's often quicker in picking up on a prospect's approval or disapproval of his sales pitch. But most of all, I find he's got more enthusiasm and energy than the fellow who's been in the business twenty years.

"I'm a great believer that the degree to which a person works depends to a great extent on just how hungry he is. The old pro who's risen to a certain level within his company and has achieved a rather comfortable lifestyle is going to sit back and enjoy that lifestyle instead of putting in the extra hours and extra effort necessary to increase his or her sales record. But a beginning salesperson still has a lot to gain by consistently improving his sales performance."

Closing the Generation Gap

"Don't talk to me about today's young people," the hard-boiled supervisor snapped. "They're only interested in getting as much pay as possible for the least amount of work!"

Maybe so, maybe not. Let's look at things through the young newcomers' eyes.

Robert Newcomb and Marg Sammons, employee communication experts, give some interesting sidelights from a survey among young new employees (from six months to a year on the job) at a small manufacturing company. As reported in the American Management Associations publication *Personnel*, the company had been baffled and disturbed by the obvious apathy and high turnover rate among this age group.

Look at some typical comments received by the survey interviewers:

"I'm strictly a number on a card."

"I came to this plant with enthusiasm, but with the exception of a few men, no one has made me feel welcome."

"They expect a day's work out of me, and that's all they'll get. They don't care about me, so why should I care about them?"

The survey revealed a sizeable communications gap, accompanied by sloppy management practices. Difficulties appeared from the word go, say Newcomb and Sammons. As one young employee put it, "I was hired with only the most hurried kind of reference check, and this made me think the company wanted only my arms and legs. The plant safety man interviewed me because the regular interviewer was too busy."

There were also complaints about vague job orientation. "I've been told the employee benefits are not good, but I also have been told they're above average," said another recently hired young fellow. "I've asked my supervisor about it, but he doesn't seem to know for sure."

Another young man said that although he found his foreman knew the technical answers about the job, there were a lot of questions about the company and its future plans that the foreman could not answer.

In the same low-morale vein, the young employees believed that there was favoritism in promotion, that the newcomer had few opportunities ahead of him. They charged that the older supervisors dampened the spirits of the younger employees. One comment: "I was all hot about this job when I first came to the company, but my foreman sure cooled any enthusiasm I had for it."

The company took the survey results to heart and instituted corrective action, including:

The personnel department is now spending much more time with each applicant. And an illustrated handbook explaining the benefit program has been prepared, tied in with a slide film shown at indoctrination sessions.

A program of frequent job reviews has been established, with special emphasis on the early days of employment.

Supervisors are now given a "tip sheet" for use at meetings with their own people, to ensure a flow of accurate information. After such meetings, the information flow is reversed by means of a supervisory reporting system.

Formal exit interviews have been instituted, so that when an employee leaves, Personnel can try to find out *why*.

A parting thought on hiring

Don't become part of the cult of resumé worshippers. The fact that somebody can log in on his resumé two or three years akin to the category we are in too often may outweigh the fact that he has actually accomplished little or nothing in that category. . . . Don't reward a resumé. A resumé can tell you where a guy's body has been for the past two years, but it doesn't tell you where his mind has been.

—*James J. Jordan, Jr.*

Training and Developing

The Look-Ahead Foreman

Foreman A (talking to a fellow foreman during a coffee break): How come I heard you advising that new youngster to study blueprint reading and mechanical drawing at night? You know he'll never need those skills on any opening likely to come up in your department, or in any department here, with those government contracts running out.

Foreman B: Maybe we won't need 'em in my department, but I want him to be as well rounded as possible when the inevitable layoff comes, so he can get a good job somewhere else.

All of us practically had to double our working force because of that government contract, so we've all added green workers and given 'em quickie training for a few simple operations. But you know and I know that this is a temporary situation. We've scraped the bottom of the barrel to get some of these greenhorns. But where I see anyone with promise, I'm advising these instant machine-tenders to take night courses to be prepared for the day when we have to lower the boom.

And if, by good luck and good sales effort, we *don't* have to lower the boom—well, I've helped produce some good people for us to use right here!

There Are No Unimportant Jobs

An industrial engineer had been retained by a large corporation to make a survey of all operations in its various plants. He was in the president's office, giving an interim oral report on his conclusions before submitting the formal report, a comprehensive volume which was in the process of being typed.

"Quite aside from my interest in the specific operational procedures and cost-cutting opportunities you wanted investigated," he was saying, "I was certainly impressed by the job that one department head, Ed Vance (and he named a particular department in a certain plant) must be doing in getting across, to *all* employees, the significance of their particular job.

"As you know, it was arranged that I talk to specific employee group representatives. In this plant, a janitor named Frank (I never got his full name, but I intend to) came to talk to me, and without any prompting, opened right up—

"'I represent the janitors,' he said. 'We believe that a clean plant is an efficient plant,' and then he went on to point out how his job also contributes to better working conditions for other workers, and how this gets translated ultimately in the production of products at lowest possible cost, and how the jobs this creates contribute to the well-being of the whole surrounding valley. He talked about the importance of his work for public relations, too, because that plant has many visitors during the course of the year, and they judge the whole company by what they see.

"One could easily conceive the janitor's job as being concerned with *dirt*. This man sees his job in terms of *cleanliness*. He sees his

202

job as playing an important role in the success of an organization with which he identifies.

"This man has a sense of self-respect because the local plant leadership has defined him as respectable. Because of the kind of supervision he has, he clearly attaches positive value to his work."

The Priceless Ingredient

"By the way," said plant manager Hal Norton at the conclusion of the weekly supervisors' meeting, "what seems to be holding up the arrangements for the retraining and transfer program? Personnel tells me they've got practically no volunteers from your departments for those aptitude tests and counseling interviews we were going to set up."

The company had undertaken a comprehensive modernization and automation program, and there were going to be a lot of changes in operations and some work-force reductions. But it looked as though, with proper handling, the new people problems could be worked out pretty well. With some training and retraining, the skills available in the plant would be entirely suitable to the new operations; and (for those who were willing to relocate) the displaced workers could be largely absorbed in other company plants. For the rest, Personnel had been active in contacting local plants for openings, subject to qualification tests and interviews.

But the rub was, in the supervisor's words answering Hal's question, there were few takers. Not many were signing up for the fairly elaborate program of psychological tests and employee counseling interviews. The personnel department was trying to set these up with the aid of a team of industrial psychologists from the local university and some employment counselors from the state employment service. While the date was rapidly approaching when the shift to the new operations would go into full gear, and there was a general feeling of uneasiness and insecurity in the air, too few of the employees seemed to want to sign up for the individual tests and interviews.

Then, amid the general shrugging of shoulders, Nat Turner spoke up. He was supervisor of one of the larger departments, and it so happened that a fair number of his people were facing displacement because of the technological changes. "I think I know what the trouble is," he said. "The whole program as announced in those mimeographed letters from Personnel and in the plant paper and on bulletin boards is too damn impersonal—and, well, *frightening* to a lot of people. All this business about aptitude tests by long-domed psychologists, and counseling programs by the state employment service that they think will pry into their personal lives."

"What do you suggest?" asked Hal.

"I think we should get Vera Anderson into the act, to do the necessary preliminary explaining and counseling, on a friendly, personal basis," replied Nat, and he went on the explain what he had in mind.

The plant manager bought Nat's idea, and it worked like a charm. Here's what they did: Vera Anderson was the plant nurse, and she had been around a long time. All the workers knew her, and they all liked and respected her. Her services went far beyond first aid, because she knew how to listen, how to keep confidences, how to come up with cheerful and encouraging words. So the manager put her in charge of all the preliminary arrangements for the testing and counseling program.

The plant cafeteria provided familiar surroundings, and with some portable partitions a corner was set off as headquarters for her preliminary counseling interviews. When the workers were told she was in charge of arrangements, they lost all of their former reluctance and suspicions. When they came to see her, she told them what the program was all about, and arranged schedules and answered questions. She gave the more timid workers confidence and the willingness to expose themselves to the strange experience of taking dexterity and general ability tests, and paper-pencil quizzes, and she knew enough about most of the jobs to be able to discuss with seasoned workers the advisability of looking into the training and retraining courses being offered. And since she knew most of the workers personally, they felt free to discuss with her some of the family and other problems involved in possible relocations.

Vera Anderson didn't lay claim to being a psychologist, and she wasn't a professional job counselor, or an expert on machine operations. But she amply supplied what Nat's intuition had told him was missing—the personal touch that made it possible for the professionals to bring their expertise to bear.

Tortoise or Hare?

Frank Richards, along with other supervisors, had been attending a series of meetings on "How to Teach a Job," conducted by a consultant who specialized in installing training programs. At the conclusion of one of the sessions, Frank raised a question that had been bothering him.

"What should I stress—*speed* or *accuracy*? Should I have new employees start at or close to the full speed and tempo of the job, and let them improve their accuracy as they get experience? Or should I have them begin in slow motion and bear down on accuracy and mistake-free work, with the idea that speed will come naturally?"

Here is how the training expert answered Frank's question:

"There are, of course, operations where you don't have any choice: for example, the speed of a machine or conveyor may be fixed and can't be reduced to accommodate the learner. But where you do have a choice, stress *smoothness* and *accuracy* as first requirements, and let speed come later.

"It's always easier to increase the rate at which a well-learned series of motions is being made than it is to try to correct bad habits acquired during the early stages, when an attempt is made to achieve accuracy and speed at the same time.

"As the worker with the accent on accuracy picks up speed, he or she will pass the fast starter in production. The latter may in fact never achieve the output of the slow starter as finally attained, and if he does reach it, he will do so only after a long and painful process of rooting out a number of bad habits that have had time to become firmly set.

"And there is always a tendency for those early bad habits to crop up from time to time under conditions of fatigue or inattention. That's a handicap the worker who has been drilled in correct work habits from the start doesn't have."

The Payoff

Situation: An industrial cleaner manufacturer has a product which is used to clean grease and oil off of concrete shop floors. During the course of using this product in one plant, a visiting serviceman discovers that the customer has found that the product is also excellent for removing grease traces from machined aluminum parts. This is a new and totally divergent use for the manufacturer's product.

Query: What does the serviceman do with this information? Does he regard it as an idle bit of trivia to be mentioned casually when he's chewing the fat with the boys back at the plant? Or does he see in it an opportunity to expand the company's sales, and see to it, either through channels or via the company's suggestion system, that the idea gets to the proper quarters for attention?

Answer: It all depends on the indoctrination he got from his supervisor.

The Sad Case of the Unnecessary Training

In a gas company, the serviceman for gas air-conditioning units had too many call-backs on the machines he was servicing. His department manager concluded that he needed more training, and sent him to a factory school for a refresher course.

Two weeks later, he returned—the star graduate—but he continued to have practically the same number of call-backs.

The department head was puzzled, but made the most of it, since the man obviously knew all there was to know about the workings of the conditioners. Worse still, he had a number of other servicemen with similar call-back trouble. Some of these were also sent to the factory school, with no better results.

Finally the company called in an industrial psychologist who was an expert in industrial training. His method was to make a systematic analysis of training *needs*, to concentrate on deficiencies and how to overcome them, rather than having employees take a broad range of training on subjects they already knew.

The answer turned out to be that the servicemen had been performing all of the complex service tasks adequately all along—except for the critical one of making sure that the air conditioners were level.

Thus, several years and many dollars after the first man had been sent to the factory school, the company discovered that more than 80 percent of its service costs had been due to the unlevel conditioners—a problem that was one of clear and specific *instruction* on a specific task, not a broad-based training need, and also clearly one of supervision. The servicemen already knew all they had to know except for that one function of leveling.

Moral: In training, don't use a shotgun instead of a rifle!

The Ordeal of Jim Foley

Jim Foley was on his way downtown to the Businessmen's Club, to take a last look at the arrangements for the quarterly supervisors' seminar to be held there all of the next day. Jim was general chairman, and he was going to open the meeting by showing a half-hour color-sound motion picture on PERT (Program Evaluation and Review Technique) which he had obtained from the Navy.

Original arrangements had been made for a man from Personnel, who knew all about visual aids, to run the projector, but now he had come down sick at the last minute, and Jim would have to run it himself, as well as doing some explanatory talking. He was a bit nervous about this, because he didn't know the first thing about motion-picture projectors. However, the Navy man had been kind enough to show him how to turn it on, how to stop it and even back it up at one point where he was to explain the relationship of an application to the plant in Brownsville, and how to shut it off at the end.

Jim was a trifle late because he had spent most of the afternoon at a special meeting on "teaching people how to teach," and he was tired and hungry, and hoped the projector had been put in place so that he could just take a quick look and go out and get some dinner before coming back to run through the film. And he was looking forward to the drink he decided he would treat himself to at dinner.

When he got to the meeting room, he breathed a sigh of relief. There, sure enough, was the projector all set up, along with the screen. And there on the table beside the projector was the can of film.

And then a cold and clammy thought struck Jim. He suddenly realized that all of the Navy man's instructions had been on how to operate the machine with the film already threaded inside it. Jim didn't have the slightest idea about how to get the film into the machine. He opened the door at the side of the projector and saw a confusing mass of pulleys and sprockets. He didn't even bother opening the can of film. With the Personnel man sick, there wasn't anyone to call. And this wasn't any little home movie. This was a monstrous affair, designed for big meetings, and the projector stared back at him with its unfriendly lens, and seemed to grow bigger as he looked at it.

Then he had an idea. He got a classified phone book and looked up the name of the biggest photographic store in town, hurried outside, and taxied over to it. Luckily it was still open. He explained his predicament to the clerk in charge of projectors, who cheerfully volunteered to stay on a few minutes after closing to show Jim how to thread film into a machine. He got a demonstration reel and threaded a projector of the same make and model as the one in Jim's meeting room.

With relief flooding over him, Jim watched the clerk go through the steps, which now looked surprisingly simple. It would be a cinch. He began to taste that drink again, and looked at his watch. It was late. The restaurant would close its doors to newcomers in fifteen minutes, although it would continue to serve the diners remaining.

"Okay," said the clerk. "You see how it's done? Just thread this end of the film through the frammy here, tighten this wingnut, give a flip to this frobidge clamp, and you're ready for business. Wanna try it once yourself?"

"No," said Jim, "I'm late for dinner. But I see it's quite simple. Thanks a million—you saved my life!" And he left to get that dry Manhattan and order a nice meal. He deserved it.

After two drinks and a leisurely full-course dinner on the expense account, Jim returned to the Club to thread his projector and call it a night.

He whistled to himself as he took the film out of the can, and confidently opened the door of the projector.

And then—*holy smoke!* He couldn't remember what the clerk

had done after he threaded the end through the frammy—if indeed this was the frammy. And then he couldn't figure out how to get the film between two metal clamps (were they frobidge clamps?) just behind the lens. He was certain that the clerk had threaded the film between them, since the film certainly had to pass the lens. Only someone seemed to have welded these two together.

Jim struggled with his problem for two solid hours, with cold sweat breaking out over him. He visualized all those people at his meeting tomorrow, with him standing there, unable even to get his film into the projector. And now he couldn't even remember what he was going to say at that point where he was to stop the machine and back it up.

And then, almost at midnight, it happened. He pushed a certain little doohickey, and the frobidge clamps opened! That was it. He remembered now that at one stage of the procedure the clerk had actually pointed out this little doohickey.

Jim threaded his film, and staggered out to the parking lot to his car. It would be one o'clock before he got home.

As he was driving home, it suddenly dawned upon him that what he had gone through—rather, what he had neglected to do—was exactly what the seminar leader at that afternoon's training session had made such a point of: *the performance tryout*.

Jim swore a mighty oath. From this point on he would be the best damn on-the-job-training performer the company ever had. He went contentedly to bed. The lesson he had learned was worth the ordeal.

The Frame-Up

"Joe," said the v.p. to his assistant, "how come Frank Wellman over in building A has such a good record with that group of disadvantaged trainees we gave him, while other supervisors seem to be having problems? He hasn't had a single dropout, while the quit rate in some of the other departments has been fantastic."

"I've noticed Frank's record, too," replied Joe. "I'm definitely going to check into it, and I'll report back."

(The company had hired a rather large number of people from the ghetto groups as part of a drive to better the economic condition of the poor in its community—a large eastern city.)

A few days later, Joe had at least one of the answers for the v.p.:

"It seems to boil down to the simple fact that Frank takes a *personal interest* in those trainees. He's actually been in some of their homes—on invitation.

"Incidentally, in doing that, he found that less than one in ten of those people in their neighborhoods have a recent photograph of themselves in their homes. And the photos he did see hardly ever reflected any competitive achievement.

"So—all on his own—Frank arranged for every ghetto trainee assigned to one of his departments to be photographed in training soon after he enters the program. He conned our model shop fellows to frame these photographs after hours, and they are then presented to the trainee. The pictures show the worker in his role as a trainee and then as a qualified worker. The men and women take these pictures home, and many hang them on their living-

215

room wall. In Frank's words, 'That picture in the home reinforces the trainee's daily image of himself or herself as a worker'—

"And remember, Chief, I don't think Frank ever had a course in psychology in his life. He apparently doesn't need one!"

While Joe was talking, the v.p. was jotting a name on his calendar pad. "By the way," he said, "I'm going to make it my business to have a little talk with Frank this week. I'd like to get to know him a little better."

Insurance Against Downtime

"I already knew from our production control records that Chuck Wilson was running a highly efficient department," remarked the head of Industrial Engineering, "but I had never had occasion to wonder just why that was.

"But it was amply borne in on me one day when I was asked to make a special check of a certain high-speed stapling operation in the odd-size cartoning line. I went over there myself because the union had made a big point about reclassifying it upward.

"I talked to Ted Kramer, who was the operator on that particular machine. The machine and associated equipment accommodated runs over a wide range of sizes and shapes, imprinted special lettering on the sides of the cartons, automatically recorded weights, and shunted various classes of boxes onto different roller-conveyor paths.

"At first glance, the operation seemed quite complicated, but Ted had it well under control.

"The point that impressed me was that during the next half-hour, Ted told me more about automatic carton filling than I thought there was to know. He showed how various undesirable results would occur if he or one of the women were careless. He pulled the manufacturer's catalog and instruction books from a cabinet shelf and referred to diagrams, pointing out the parts that had to be replaced frequently, and certain electronic controls that would go haywire if abused. He explained that he himself made all minor repairs to the equipment.

"All in all, Ted Kramer gave me a convincing demonstration of an operator who knew his machine, knew its shortcomings, knew how to operate it properly and to keep it in good running order. He definitely had a lot of *job pride*.

"I could see that Chuck Wilson had certainly done a good job of instruction, or at least had stimulated Ted to learn all he could about his machine. In any event, *this man knew his job*.

"That was the secret of Chuck's outstanding record of practically no downtime or equipment emergencies. Undoubtedly, every other operator in his department knew his job thoroughly.

"Of course, we don't expect all equipment operators to make minor repairs, as Ted did (even if the union permitted it). But Ted was certainly a better automatic carton line operator because he had studied his machine."

Do You Talk Safety or Teach It?

Foreman True White and foreman Bart Black, both old-time line bosses with the same company, are considered experts in directing their work crews to get a job done. But there is one great difference in their performance records: while True's crew consistently captures the company safety award year after year, Bart's crew just as consistently turns in a poor safety record.

Each crew does similar work, and each draws its men from the same community. Furthermore, each foreman has about the same experience and capability as the other. So how do you explain the wide difference in their safety records? There has to be something Bart is overlooking and True is practicing.

The difference is that True, with the best company safety record, long ago stopped *talking about* safety as a substitute for actual *job instruction.* He makes sure each of his men knows the proper way to do his job. Bart talks about *safety,* but doesn't talk enough about *job skills.* Instead of merely telling his men to work safely, True takes the time to instruct them on proper handling of tools, operation of machines, maintenance and housekeeping routines, and just plain good work attitudes—all things that Bart neglects.

True knows that proper work habits, good operating practices, and common sense cover much more ground than the *word* safety. You can't tell a maintenance engineer to "oil that machine safely," or a truck driver to "drive safely," or a tractor operator to "operate safely," or a crane rigger to "rig safely," and expect good results unless the engineer is taught the machine's operation, the truck driver how to drive and park a rig, the tractor man how to drive his machine correctly, the rigger how to handle cables and weights.

Bart "talks safety." Foreman True White teaches good work habits to his crew, and trains them, or sees that they are trained, to do specific jobs.*

* Based on "A Tale of Two Masters" in *The Channel*, an accident prevention publication of the Pacific Maritime Association.

Show Biz

Going in for dramatics can do a lot to drive the safety message home. For example, when one safety engineer toured a plant, he took along styrofoam hands so that he could demonstrate how fast a finger could be chopped off.

At a chemical plant, men were asked to don goggles with blank metal plates for lenses. For thirty sightless minutes they were asked to identify the contents of large envelopes, distinguish between different denominations of money, light a cigarette, sign a blank check, count dots on a Braille card. After that, they were no longer "in the dark" as regards a healthy respect for eyes and eye protection.

A foreman in a machining department secured a glass eye from the safety department and carried it around in his pocket, producing it with appropriate comments whenever he discussed eye protection with his people.

In one plant, the subject scheduled for a safety discussion was "Hard Hats." As part of the presentation, the men were grouped around a compression testing machine to show just how much punishment a hard hat would take. A small prize was offered for the closest guess as to how much resistance strength a hard hat has.

Rating Performance?
Be Specific!

"I'm not satisfied with the appraisal and progress reports you fellows have been turning in on your people," the plant manager said as an opener for the weekly supervisory meeting. "I sampled quite a few of them with Thatcher (the plant personnel manager), and I agree with him that they're definitely not specific enough to serve any useful purpose.

"Fortunately, we got some dividends from Joe Norton's attending that management society seminar last week. He brought some sample rating forms back with him, and with some slight changes I had Thatch reproduce them for our use. Pass 'em out, Joe."

Joe handed out sets of three forms (shown on the following pages), and the rest of the meeting was spent discussing their use.

Note how the forms spell out *definite gradations of performance* in *specified areas of job requirements*. One big advantage of these forms is that all supervisors and all workers can "talk the same language" when it comes time for "how am I doing?" discussions. Note also that with slight adaptations, forms like these can be used for office as well as plant, and in fact for retailing and other service operations too.

This is your merit rating for —

OUTPUT

It Covers:
(1) Dependability on the job, not absent, tardy, or wasting time.
(2) Putting out, not holding back.
(3) Willingness to do any job available.
(4) Teamwork and extra effort in case of absence of others of in emergencies.

This rating is done by your department head jointly with Production Control in the shop and with other department heads in the office and engineering.

NAME

Outstanding.

Very dependable on the job, does all the work he can, very good in teamwork and meeting emergencies.

Dependable, does not hold back, tries to maintain output by teamwork and extra effort when needed.

Usually dependable and on the job. Does not hold back, fair teamworker.

Does a days work, will try other jobs and occasionally helps in emergencies.

Wastes time occasionally, holds back some, does other jobs when out of work reluctantly.

Wastes time, holds back.

This is your merit rating for —

WORKMANSHIP
AND ATTITUDE
TOWARD QUALITY

It Covers:
(1) The quality of work produced.
(2) The elimination of scrap.
(3) The elimination of errors.
(4) Your attitude toward improving quality of our finished product.

This rating is done by your department head jointly with Inspection in the shop and with other department heads in the office and engineering.

NAME

Outstanding.

Work is superior, minimum quality supervision necessary.

Quality of work is good. Tries to improve quality.

Slightly above fair quality.

Workmanship is of a fair quality, occasional errors, makes some scrap.

Quality sometimes unsatisfactory, makes scrap and errors.

Poor quality, too much scrap, too many errors, attitude needs improvement.

This is your merit rating for —

SUPERVISION
REQUIRED

It Covers:
(1) Knowledge of your job and helpfulness by imparting it to others.
(2) Your ability to supervise yourself.
(3) Your initiative and all around skill.
(4) Your orderliness and care of equipment.

This rating has been done by your department head.

NAME	
	Outstanding.
	Unusual job knowledge on his and other jobs. Helpful to others, requires no supervision, takes pride in equipment and work station.
	Expert on job, does help others, requires little supervision, careful of equipment and orderly.
	Considerable job knowledge, requires some supervision, takes some initiative, orderly and careful of equipment.
	Has required job knowledge, requires supervision, can do other jobs, is fairly orderly, gives equipment fair care.
	Lacks required job knowledge, needs supervision. Not orderly. May give equipment poor care.
	Requires additional training and experience, needs supervision regularly, apt not to take care of equipment.

Rx for Identifying Management Potential

The Cincinnati service manager of Pitney Bowes has a special kind of reputation. His service department is first in its division under the company's quota and scoring system. The branch as a whole, which has been a consistent winner over the years, is currently running second among the top twenty-three in the company.

But the special thing about Bill Dirr, thirty years with Pitney Bowes and Cincinnati's service chief since 1961, is that his particular branch has "graduated" into other field-sales offices no less than five successful service managers and two field-service managers. As far as anyone at PB knows, that's a record.

As managers and supervisors, all of us obviously have something to learn from Bill. Especially since, in addition to his "graduates," Bill says that "right now there are four people I could recommend for promotion to field-service manager some place."

Dirr's rationale for the presence of so much good managerial material in his branch ranges from training, discipline, goal setting, and crystal-clear communication, to just plain good fortune. As to "good fortune," he says, "You have to have the right people, and we've been lucky. I think we have one of the best service groups in the U.S. They're self-starters, their attitudes are good, they respect decisions, they're company people.

"They're concerned about everything. We work together; you don't think of yourself as boss. The confidence and desire for management status just grows in that kind of soil. It really boils down to hiring the right person to start with."

226

But hiring the right people to start with is more than "good fortune." Selection procedures in Cincinnati Service are lengthy and thorough. Interviews with field-service managers and Dirr himself run to a total of four or five hours, and the applicants are observed as they relate to their prospective coworkers in Sales and Administration as well as Service. Tours of the building, and field trips with qualified observers are part of the selection process.

Over the years Dirr has released only five people. He regards these as his personal failures. "I kept them on too long, trying to make it work, but it started to affect the others," he says regretfully.

Here is Dirr's Rx for identifying management potential: "You watch them work, listen when they talk to you, see whether others turn to them for answers. Attitude is everything. The person with potential doesn't complain or alibi. He has self-control, rapport with the others. Beyond that, the best you can do for him is make sure he knows what's expected—and set a good example. It will rub off."

An interviewer for PB's employee newspaper asked Dirr to analyze the service managers who once worked for him. His dissection of the composite of the group is, in effect, a checklist of successful management style:

"He always got the job done. He couldn't stand idleness. Everything was go, go, go. Although when necessary he would work twelve hours a day, his 'management style' was to work smarter, not harder.

"He would make sure that the guys went right to their first customer in the A.M. without wasting time coming into the office. He'd analyze the reasons for call-backs, give the representative the additional training that would cut down on all call-backs.

"A pusher. Dynamic—a driver, but fair. He didn't bug people.

"Aggressive, patient, and friendly. A motivator."

Dirr doesn't deny the importance of money, but he discounts it as the prime motivator. He believes strongly in *self*-motivation. "Again, it's attitude, and whether the person likes the job. When a rep likes his job, he's on his toes and interested in everything. He makes things happen that keep the job interesting. All that time he's forming the kind of reactions and responses that make him a superior employee—or manager.

"When we hire someone new, I always tell him, 'When the day comes that your job really seems like work, and when you hate to start the day, that's the time to change jobs.'"

A parting thought on training

A little arithmetic will demonstrate the importance of the supervisor in training: Allowing for two weeks' vacation, an individual employee spends about 2,000 hours per year at work. In some companies, 40 of these hours may be spent in formal training activities. This leaves 1,960 hours per year when the employee's experience will be directed by his supervisor and not by a training person. Even without considering that the supervisor is the employee's boss and is thus in a naturally influential position, the training person in 40 hours could not be expected to have an impact equal to that which a supervisor could develop in 1,960 hours.

—from a Kraft Foods Company
statement of its training philosophy

Rules and Regulations

Mirror, Mirror on the Wall—
Who Is the Fairest One of All?

Remembering the above rhyme from Snow White (a favorite tale of his young daughter's —he'd read it to her dozens of times) enabled supervisor Ned Firmer to tighten up his department's adherence to company rules about neatness and personal appearance, without hurting anyone's feelings.

Ned had a lot of women working for him in the three departments under his jurisdiction. And what with stepped-up business and the addition of certain assembly operations, his force had almost doubled over the past year.

The trouble was that he had become acutely aware of a general falling-off in personal appearance and "tone." He thought that maybe Personnel, in order to fill recruitment requisitions, hadn't been able to be as choosy as it normally was. At any rate, a large number of the women seemed to be wearing spotty dresses, others were prone to walk about with their slips showing and looking untidy in one way or another. This was especially serious in Ned's case, because his operations were ones that a lot of customers and prospects wanted to see, in order to get a first-hand look at the kind of work being turned out.

For some time Ned thought about the advisability of bringing these shortcomings to the attention of the individuals who seemed to be the worst offenders, but he didn't want to stir up a hornet's nest. Besides, the problem was one of general laxness—bluntly, an impression of overall sloppiness—not specific glaring defects that

233

you could make a big fuss over. He also considered issuing an impersonal memo on the subject of personal neatness, calling attention to the page and a half devoted to the subject in the company's rule book issued to every employee, but he didn't think that would do much good. He suggested the idea of snappy, attractive smocks or uniforms to the plant manager, but was turned down for budgetary reasons.

Then Ned had a bright idea, involving a bit of practical psychology. He couldn't get a couple of thousand dollars for smocks, but he was able to wangle the much smaller sum needed for his experiment.

He had two good-quality full-length mirrors installed in the lounge used by the women in his departments. There was an immediate improvement in the looks of all concerned.

They Police Themselves

"What are your rules about coffee breaks and the use of this fine employees' lounge?" a writer from a trade magazine asked the president of a company who was showing him around the company's brand new offices. The floors had no partitions; all offices were "open," merely separated by potted plants, attractive small movable partitions, and arrangements of beautifully designed bookcases, cabinets, and the like. This was the new (at that time) "Office Landscape" concept, and the magazine was going to run a feature story on it.

"We don't have any fixed coffee breaks, and the employees are free to leave their work places and take a breather in the lounge whenever they want to," the president explained. (The lounge, like all of the other areas, including the executive "offices"—also open spaces—was in full view of anyone passing.) "The only rule is that no coffee or other beverages, or food or candy, can be consumed at the work places. We're too proud of our wall-to-wall carpeting and other decor to take a chance on spillage."

"No rules at all?" exclaimed the writer incredulously. "How do you prevent abuse of the privilege—people goofing off any time they feel like it?"

"*We* don't prevent the abuse," said the president. "*The employees themselves* do it, merely by the force of 'public opinion' and the inherent self-respect that makes people want to preserve a good image of themselves. A psychologist-consultant advised us to establish this policy when we went into 'Office Landscaping,' and it's worked. When employees know that they're in full view of

235

everyone when they leave their work place, and anyone passing by can see them reading or smoking or chatting in the lounge, they make it a point not to abuse the privilege.

"Public view of a person's action is the best policeman in the world, and he's not even on the payroll!"

You've Got to Mean It

Sports commentator Red Barber has a favorite story he has often told over the air. It concerns the coach who gave very explicit instructions to the rookie player not to try to steal second in a critical inning. To the coach's dismay, the rookie completely ignored his injunctions. He tried for second and predictably got caught in the middle—and was tagged out.

Back in the dugout, the coach chewed the young player out with appropriately pungent "expletives deleted."

"I told you and *told* you not to steal second. *Why in the blankety blank blank did you do it#@!!##??*"

The kid looked at him in wide-eyed innocence, and said, in a tone indicating a conviction that he was offering a completely reasonable explanation, "Coach, I just didn't think you meant it."

That attitude may be at the heart of a manager's problem with respect to getting his people to adhere to company policies, rules, and regulations—minor infractions here and there, in, say, clocking in on time, or obeying "no smoking" signs, or in housekeeping, or in necessary paperwork. None of these may be overly serious by itself, but all add up to a general impression of laxity in supervision. And unlike the case of Red Barber's coach, the fault actually lies with the manager himself.

"I didn't think you meant it" is an almost inevitable consequence of inconsistent concern about rules—blowing hot one day and cool the next, or of inconsistent treatment of individuals—cracking down hard on some infractors and shrugging shoulders about others, or fuzziness in explaining rules, especially to newcomers, or even a lack of knowledge or understanding on the manager's part about what *does* consitute the company's official position on a given matter.

All of which doesn't mean that a manager must go so strictly by the book as to preclude any exceptions for unusual and meritorious reasons. But these must be treated *as* exceptions, and carefully publicized as such.

Query: How taut a ship are *you* running?

No Language Barrier Here!

"It's about time we got out a new edition of our employee booklet of rules and regulations and special safety precautions, isn't it?" the head of a medium-sized manufacturing plant said to his manufacturing manager.

"You're right, J.B.," said the manufacturing manager. "But this time I've got a better idea. The way to get those pointers across is to speak the employees' language."

"Hasn't it always been in English?" the president wanted to know.

"Sure, but not in *their* kind of English. Here's my idea this time," and he outlined a new procedure. The president bought it right off. Here's what the plant manager did:

The foremen in all departments were asked to get ideas about workable rules and regulations from the people in their department, with special emphasis on safety hazards and precautions. The foremen were called together in a meeting, after the forms for employee suggestions had been distributed, and were asked to select three of their number to be responsible for weeding out duplications, and for the final recommended wording of the rules, making necessary additions where there were omissions from management's point of view.

The foremen's draft was submitted to the personnel department. The head of Personnel did only slight editing, to make the wording grammatically consistent. (But not *too* grammatical! If, for example, the boys split an infinitive, or were a little repetitious here and there, the wording was allowed to stand. And on style, the personnel director even allowed expressions like *Be damn careful here!* to remain to emphasize certain safety pointers, as well as *Don't be a damn fool!* on a rule having to do with horseplay.)

Coffee Break (and All Such)

Memo posted at Papas Refrigeration Company:

TO ALL EMPLOYEES: Due to increased competition and a desire to stay in business, we find it necessary to institute a new policy. We are asking that somewhere between starting and quitting time, and without infringing too much on the time usually devoted to Lunch Periods, Coffee Breaks, Rest Periods, Story Telling, Ticket Selling, Vacation Planning, and the Rehashing of Yesterday's TV Programs, each employee endeavor to find some time that can be set aside and be known as the "Work Break."*

* Item in the *Houston Post*.

The Efficient In-Between

"Somewhere between the 'let's-fire-him' and the 'take-it-easy-on-him' types of supervisors," remarked a vice president of Manufacturing at a management-society luncheon meeting, "there just have to be those who understand that discipline is *a means to an end*—a tool to be used in the hands of a professional. Proper use of the tool helps develop an efficient, well-functioning group. On the other hand, even a hammer and a nail in the hands of someone who doesn't know how to use them will result in marring the wood and smashing the finger.

"Probably, in a company as big as ours, it's inevitable that we are going to have supervisors who fit the two opposite types. The one extreme believes in meting out harsh and frequent penalties. He uses his rank, his position, and his authority in an effort to shorten the route to his objectives. By using discipline in this manner, people can be frightened into avoiding any situation that could result in disciplinary action. Out of fear they exercise no independent judgment, take no action on their own, and hesitate when they should be decisive.

"On the other extreme is the supervisor who thinks efficiency and cooperation can be bought with leniency. He believes that by removing the restraints on employees, resentment is eliminated. And this is probably true. *But* lack of discipline results in carelessness and negligence."

That vice president must have been reading our mail!

242

A parting thought on discipline

The ship was famous in the Pacific Fleet a few years before World War II. Her captain was a man with a negative attitude toward life. His instinctive response to a proposal of any kind was a strong and decided "NO!," and the general announcing system was kept busy day and night in passing out information that reflected his character:

"There will *be no* liberty."

"There will *be no* four-o'clock boat."

"There will *be no* men out of uniform on the weather decks."

"There will *be no*. . . ."

She was known, quite simply, as the Be-No Ship.

Nearby was another ship of the same class. Her captain was no Pollyanna, no spreader of good cheer for good cheer's sake; but he had a positive attitude toward his command, and he possessed the happy faculty of phrasing his wishes in a way that made his officers and men understand them and execute them cheerfully.

If his ship entered port at 2:00 A.M., there would be liberty, and though only the married men showed any desire to go ashore at that hour, the others were content in the knowledge that they could leave the ship if they wanted to. This ship was known as the Can-Do ship.

—Rear Admiral Frederick J. Bell, USN (Retired),
vice president, Flood and Watson, Inc.,
in *The Management Review*

Critical Incidents

How to Handle a Critical Incident

"I know one big reason now why Jack Kilmar got that vice president job," remarked a management consultant in discussing a client company's affairs with his colleagues. "I got an insight into his mode of operating with people when I was in his office the other day."

"What happened?" he was asked.

The consultant explained as follows:

We were discussing how to get out of that production snafu they got into with their supplier, United Fabricators. As you know, Joe Eager, the production foreman Jack promoted to be project manager for that new-model Fraggle-Former they're pushing through, did some high-pressure personal expediting with UF to get his frame deliveries two weeks earlier than contracted for. He laid it on the line about the dire need to pick up that extra time to keep his project on schedule. UF obliged, but deliveries on three other projects are now snarled up, and a lot of people are screaming for Joe's head.

While I was in Jack's office, Harry Ewing, head of Engineering, and that new vice president who's head of General Contracts came storming in. There are no two ways about it—Joe Eager was out of line. The new v.p.'s nose was out of joint because Joe had bypassed him on the UF rescheduling and claimed Joe just didn't know how to work in a big organization. Harry Ewing fumed about too much Joe "Eager-Beavering" on a lot of things. "He's one man we can do without around here," he said. "Maybe you can't fire him out of hand, but let me tell you, we'll all be a lot better off if you ease him out of the picture just as soon as possible!"

Jack let 'em blow off all the steam they wanted to. He gave them full sympathy. While he didn't chime in with them to lay the blame on Joe, he nodded in the right places and said he was dropping everything else to get things straightened out immediately.

When they had left, I offered to leave and to continue our conference next day. "If you're gonna call Joe Eager in here," I said, "I'd just as soon miss the fireworks."

"Sit down," said Jack. "I'm not going to call Joe in here until tomorrow morning."

"But those two guys were pretty hot," I said. "And we'll have to hold off on the details of our new approach if you're pulling Joe off the job."

"Listen," said Jack, "I'm not pulling Joe off the job." And he showed me a pad on which he'd been taking notes while his two visitors had been talking.

"Those fellows thought I was taking notes on what they were saying, but I was really jotting down some things I know about Joe Eager."

The pad had two columns, one headed with a plus sign, and one with a minus sign. Under the minus sign I noticed, "Crowds people . . . tends to forget big picture . . . sometimes too Cocky." Under the plus sign he had jotted, "Enthusiastic . . . loyal . . . ambitious—night sch. coll. grad. . . . got us out of that Wheelfax jam last May. . . . his people knock themselves out for him. . . . worked around the clock to help Ewing out of one of Ewing's own goofs."

"This UF flap is really serious," Jack commented while I was reading his notes. "Our Fraggle-Former will sure enough be on time, but Ewing's budget may now overrun $50,000 because of a penalty clause we've now got to lick with overtime and subcontracting, and our new v.p., Fred Lobyer, is going to have to commute between here and Washington for the next three weeks to smooth things over. You may not have thought it, but believe me, I had a slow but increasing burn about Joe's goof until the minute those two fellows came in."

"You mean *they* cooled you off?" I exclaimed.

"Well, they came on so strong," he replied, "that I instinctively said to myself, 'Hey, wait a minute'—and I began jotting down those pro and con pointers. Joe's a good man, and we've got a lot invested in him. Damned if I'm gonna lose his potential because of this one episode. And I'm definitely not going to call him in while he and everyone else, including me, are so hot about it." He picked up the phone, and asked his secretary to get Joe Eager on the wire. Here's how his end of the conversation went.

"Joe? . . . I see by the reports that the Fraggle-Former is back on schedule. Good work on that end. . . . [pause] But Joe—I guess you've heard [understatement of the year, and Jack winked at me!] that we're having some other scheduling problems with Harry, and Mr. Lobyer seems a bit disturbed [deadpan]. . . . Look, Joe, next time you run into a problem like this, there are some different approaches you might want to consider. Drop in here at 9:30 tomorrow, and let's see what we can learn from this whole thing."

The Case of the Impatient Foreman

Fred Underwood was hopping up and down with impatience. He was already behind schedule in his department when one of the key lines was shut down because the driving motor apparently had developed some shorted coils. He hovered around the two maintenance men on the job, and asked anxious questions about how long it would take to fix the trouble. All he got was some noncommittal grunts, and something to the effect that some broken screw heads were making it difficult to get at the thingamabob behind the whatsit.

Disgusted, Fred went to lunch. When he came back, the machine was no nearer being repaired, and what was worse, one of the electricians was gone and the other was lolling against a pillar, with his hands in his pockets.

Fred blew up. "My maintenance charges are high enough without my having to swallow time for guys holding up a pillar. Where's Ed? What's taking you guys so long? I'm gonna call Mike and see if he can't supervise these maintenance jobs better." (Mike was head of Maintenance.)

No sooner had Fred stormed off than Ed, the electrician, drove up on an electric truck with a new motor, and before long everything was in working order.

But Fred paid for his outburst for a long time. It seems the electrician had been called off the job by his own boss on an emergency matter, and had gone out of his way to tote up the motor himself,
250

to save time. He didn't take kindly to having his boss later ask him what he had done to rile up the foreman of an operating department. For some time thereafter, whenever Fred had occasion to call for some electrical work, it always seemed to turn out that a lot of rush jobs came ahead of his, and that when the jobs were done, a lot of necessary extras were always discovered that had to be done for preventive measures, so that the jobs took longer and cost more. Fred realized that he was being had, but since he couldn't point his finger at anything specific, he had to take it.

The Case of the Interrupted Overtime

In a building materials plant one day, Ed Handler got into an argument with his foreman over supper money. Ed claimed he was entitled to $5.00 because he was scheduled for twelve continuous hours. The foreman didn't agree, and refused to authorize the payment. So Ed stopped work after the tenth hour and announced that he wasn't going to do any more work that day. The foreman was furious, and in front of some of the others said, "If you won't do the work, I'll get someone who will."

Ed went home anyway, and the foreman began looking for a substitute, but no one was available for the work. The next morning Ed found his card pulled from the timeclock. He made inquiries at the front office, and found he was punished with a one-day suspension for insubordination.

"You know the union rules," the plant superintendent told him. "You're supposed to follow orders. If you thought you had a grievance, you could have filed one the next day. Walking off the job is serious. If it weren't for your good record, you'd have gotten more than a one-day suspension."

Ed wasn't satisfied, and filed a grievance. The case went to arbitration.

The union won. Why?

Management lost out because the foreman's statement ("I'll get someone who will") gave Ed reason to believe, he said, that no penalty would result from going home. Witnesses testified to the foreman's remark. Wrote the arbitrator, "There is nothing in the evidence to show that the foreman made it clear that if he could not find anyone else, Handler would have to stay and do the work assigned, and that refusal would be regarded as insubordination."*

* Based on a case from the files of the American Arbitration Association.

The Case of the Rejected Manual*

Like many other large corporations, the Ferris Magnetron Company consists of many divisions, each of which may at some time be a customer of another division. The opportunities for pressure situations are obvious.

I was responsible for preparing a technical manual on electronic test equipment for the Special Magnetic Devices Division (SMD) of Ferris. SMD was to review the manual and submit it to the U.S. Navy personnel for final acceptance. Roughly a month before scheduled delivery, a progress review meeting was held with SMD representatives. I told them the manual was incomplete and could not be submitted on schedule without large areas of missing information. They said to deliver it with whatever additional information would be available, subject to the later inclusion of the missing data, to be outlined in an accompanying memo. I agreed.

However, just before the scheduled delivery, I was sent out of town. While I was away, SMD called my boss and demanded that the manual be delivered immediately. He complied—but there was no explanatory memorandum *re* missing portions.

Two weeks later we received through top-management channels a letter from SMD, rejecting the manual. With the letter was

---

*This and the following two scenarios are first-hand accounts by members of a Critical Incident Seminar conducted by the author. Names have been changed, but not the facts.

an attachment listing about a hundred pointed comments, most of which concerned the missing information.

I felt double-crossed. The following factors complicated the situation:

1. The man who signed the letter of rejection was a personal friend of mine. He claimed he merely signed the letter without understanding its importance.
2. The pride of my people who had prepared the manual was hurt. They felt the rejection was unwarranted and demanded some counter action by me.
3. Our division was looking for more work from SMD, and did not want to antagonize them.
4. The attendant publicity was derogatory, and there was little room to "save face" short of open battle with SMD.

After many hours of meetings, the missing information was supplied and accepted, and the matter was closed. But the time spent on the meetings caused the job to overrun the budget.

My first mistake was at the initial progress review meeting. I should have refused to deliver incomplete material without clearing through top-division management. The second mistake was in not informing my boss, prior to my business trip, of the status of the manual. My third mistake was letting my personal feelings toward a friend retard action I would otherwise have taken sooner. My loyalties were divided, but the most important loyalty should have been to the good name of my working group.

The Case of the Unhappy Boss

I was responsible for a section of an airplane that my company was fabricating. This particular portion of the plane was subcontracted to another company some distance from the home plant. Tools and fixtures were shipped to this subcontractor, and I was sent to monitor the fabrication of the part, including the setting-up of the fixtures at the subcontractor's plant.

Upon uncrating the fixture, I found it to have been damaged during shipment. It would require some work to repair it, but the subcontractor's personnel could do the job. Accordingly, I authorized the repair, which was finished in a day and a half—at a cost, however, of twelve man-days of work. I reported to my superior by telephone that the fixture was repaired and things were proceeding satisfactorily.

To my surprise, instead of receiving commendation for handling a difficult situation, I found that the boss was quite upset at learning that the part had been repaired, and that in no uncertain terms he wanted immediate action on establishing blame for the damage. He made it very clear that he didn't think I should have accepted the recommendation that the repair be made until responsibility for the damage was fixed, and that I should have informed him immediately when the damage was discovered, not after it was repaired.

NOTE: Discussion of this case centered on the fact that there was obviously a question as to the limit of authority, and that the inci-

dent pointed up the difference in attitude of a person who has the "management" point of view and a person who has the "project" point of view. It was emphasized that every employee must find out for himself, unless very clearly instructed by his superior, just what the limits of his authority and responsibility are, and act accordingly, with full consideration of the personal relationship between himself and the person to whom he reports. In one case, a supervisor might chew out the subordinate for not making decisions and for bringing every little problem to him. Another supervisor might do just the opposite, and consider a display of unusual initiative as an affront to his position.

Moral: Know the extent of your freedom of action—and know your boss!

The Sad Experience of Mr. Crowder

A Real-Life "In-Basket" Case Study

NOTE: Many companies use the so-called "in-basket" method in supervisory and executive development courses. Each member of the group taking the course receives a sequence of memos taken from the "in-basket" of a hypothetical department head or supervisor, together with related communications of his own, covering a particular episode. The group then discusses how it would have handled the problem.

To: Mr. A. A. Quarters
cc.: Messrs F. Poor
         B. Alfred
January 4, 19—
From: A. Crowder
Subject: Approval of Changes to Company Forms

1. Central Forms Control, upon request of the Property Services Manager, have replaced the reproducible customer property record form (21883-1) without prior notice or Division approval. This action follows similar ones concerning forms and stationery items.

2. Company policy is to propose these changes in advance, through the Division Forms Control responsibility, who in turn would obtain comments from users and submit a response based on the Division's needs. We urge adherence to this policy. This will permit analysis of

258

the true total costs to the Company when a form is changed or an item is deleted from stationery stock.

3. We are investigating this change because it is our opinion that the previous study resulting in the reproducible CPR form was authentic. In the meantime, we request that form 21883-1 continue to be stocked in this Division.

Signed: A. Crowder,
      Organization & Procedures Supervisor,
      Surface Fabrication Division

To: A. Crowder
January 11, 19—
cc: Messrs. F. Poor
          B. Alfred
From: A. A. Quarters
Subject: Approval of Changes to Company Forms

1. I have looked into your complaint of Jan. 4 with regard to the above subject.
2. In view of your request, Form 21883-1 will be maintained in stock, pending the result of your investigation and further review with Mr. Poor.
3. I am much disturbed by the wider charge you made in your first paragraph, "This action follows similar ones concerning forms and stationery items." Would you please advise me specifically, at the earliest moment as to the occasions to which you refer? We cannot tolerate in our operations, now or in the future, any irresponsibility such as you charge.

Signed: A. Quarters
      Organization & Procedures Administrator

To: Mr. A. A. Quarters
Jan. 17, 19—
From: A. Crowder

1. There is no intent in my previous memorandum to arouse your concern about forms control. In the past we have verbally reported these situations directly to the people involved, the analysts, and yourself. Forms Control has rendered valuable service to us. In this instance, we have been by-passed. I do not think this is good practice and I am

concerned about your unwillingness to accept comments from this Division in the good faith in which they are submitted.

Signed: A. Crowder,
  Organization & Procedures Supervisor,
  Surface Fabrication Division

To: A. Crowder
February 15, 19—
From: J. J. Topper
Subject: Division Operating Procedures

1. Please be advised that the responsibility for issuing the Division Operating Procedures has been transferred to the Vice President for Administration, effective March 1, 19—
2. You will continue your responsibility for publication of this manual *under the supervision of Mr. A. A. Quarters,* Organization & Procedures Administrator.

Signed: J. J. Topper, Division Manager

Comment: This sad experience illustrates how a supervisor of an operating division (Surface Fabrications) should *not* conduct dealings with the head of a central staff service (Forms Control). One of the "in-basket" group members immediately commented that "that one little ten-word sentence at the end of the first paragraph lit the fuse!" Crowder's poor judgment was compounded by the fact that his chip-on-the-shoulder memo was addressed to someone who actually had a higher organizational title. Then, in his second memorandum, when he hastened to say he had no intention of arousing Mr. Quarters' concern, he couldn't refrain from rebuking him for his "unwillingness to accept comments" rendered "in good faith." Small wonder that the boom was lowered in memorandum no. 4.

Prescription by the group: Whenever you write a memo to get something off your chest, always reread it with yourself in the other fellow's shoes. Then tear it up, count ten, and write a better one.

A parting thought on critical incidents

A young French officer was taking advanced war-college training. At a social function he was introduced to Napoleon, and seized upon this as a wonderful opportunity to get some sound advice on a strategy problem that has been assigned to him.

"Sire," he said, "you are acknowledged to be the greatest military genius of our age. Perhaps you could enlighten me as to your strategy if you were confronted with the following situation—," and he outlined the essentials of the problem.

"Sir," replied Napoleon, "my genius consists in never allowing myself to get into such a situation in the first place!"

Exits

Court of Last Resort

"What we need around here is a 'Court of Last Resort,'" said Jim Fisher at a weekly supervisory planning session. The company employed a lot of women on its assembly operations. The work wasn't highly skilled, but it did demand a familiarity with the job so that easily made mistakes would be avoided and rejects kept down. The discharge rate was high and, what was worse, was unpredictable and spotty. Some supervisors seemed to be having more trouble than others in developing good, careful workers who were worth keeping on the job. At this meeting, the whole subject had again come up for airing.

The plant manager asked Jim to elaborate on his "court of last resort" idea, and the others at the meeting bought it. Here is the procedure they set up:

A foreman cannot dismiss any of his employees. If he is dissatisfied with one of them, he reports her to the "court of last resort," which consists of the foreman's own immediate superior and the superintendent or assistant superintendent of the division. If, after talking the matter over with the foreman, the "court" finds sufficient grounds, it notifies the plant employment manager.

But this doesn't mean that the worker is dropped from the payroll. The worker who has not made good is tried on at least three different kinds of job, and sometimes more, in an effort to fit her in successfully somewhere.

This procedure makes every woman feel that she will always be treated with justice and that if there is congenial work for her somewhere in the company, she will have a chance at it.

When there is no other course but to dismiss a worker, the employment manager does the dismissing. Of course, complete records are kept; and if it is found that some particular foreman has an unusual amount of trouble with those under him, the matter is looked into. "Habitual dismissers" are not wanted as foremen.

The Case of the Buck-Passing Foremen

In all his years as a foreman, Tom Wharton never felt as bad about having to recommend discharge as he did in the case of Mrs. B. Except for one thing, Mrs. B. was an ideal worker. She was pleasant, polite, and anxious to please, and her attendance was nearly perfect. But she simply was not bright! In eleven years with the company she had never done anything but the easiest tasks, and even so, her work was barely passable.

Over and over, Mrs. B. would be assigned to a department for a while until the foreman felt he couldn't stand her incompetence any longer. But instead of discharging her, the routine was to pass her along to some other supervisor who could somehow be talked into giving her another chance. The personnel department always okayed the move.

At the time of the discharge which finally took place, Mrs. B. was a factory clerk working part of every day under Tom's direction. All she had to do was make entries of parts numbers on ledger sheets and, after a few simple additions, enter the totals in a record book. But Mrs. B. was both slow and inaccurate. Tom spoke to her about it—gently, of course, because she was so agreeable, and she *was* trying—but nothing seemed to help. The straw that broke the camel's back came when an inventory showed a shortage of a thousand parts. Closer examination showed no shortage at all, just some more of Mrs. B.'s inaccurate records.

By this time, no other supervisor would accept her. So Tom recommended discharge, and Personnel acted on his request.

267

In view of the eleven-year record, management expressed surprise when the union filed a grievance. "Are you going to pretend Mrs. B. is a capable worker?" the personnel manager asked the shop steward.

"We're not pretending anything and we're not admitting anything," replied the steward. "But we've got you on one thing—Mrs. B. was never given the three-day layoff that should always come before discharge. For that reason alone, the dismissal is improper."

The personnel manager didn't deny that a step in the discipline procedure had been bypassed. "What would have been the point?" he asked. "Suspension is an effective form of discipline because it puts an employee on notice that unless he or she improves, he'll be fired. Actually, Mrs. B. has been on notice for years. It would have been cruel to suspend her first and then fire her."

The union refused to yield, the case worked its way through the grievance procedure, and it finally went to arbitration, using the facilities of the American Arbitration Association as provided by the contract.

The company won. The arbitrator ruled that the company had established its right to discharge. However, he did have some harsh words about the essential cruelty, despite good intentions, of "shunting from foreman to foreman" an employee who, for her own good, should have been discharged years ago. "It was clearly evident," he wrote, "that the employee was endeavoring to do her best but was obviously incapable of adequately performing her duties." He stressed that it was "neither fittingly considerate nor especially conducive to good labor relations" to subject Mrs. B. to the constant humiliation of criticism and transfers.

"Foreman after foreman simply passed the buck," he wrote, "each seeking to avoid the unpleasant task of facing up to reality in the case of an earnest and sensitive employee who was doing her level best to make good, but who nonetheless was *never* a satisfactory factory clerk and was never destined for such a role."*

NOTE: AAA offers the following comments for consideration in a post-mortem of Mrs. B.'s case:

Under most union contracts, and in the practice of most companies with or without union contracts, the first thirty days of

* Based on a case from its files supplied by the American Arbitration Association.

employment are a probationary period. *It is during this time that foremen are expected to weed out those who lack ability or have other undesirable characteristics.*

But when an employee is hired for a job that requires minimal ability, as Mrs. B. apparently was, almost any employee is good enough for the first thirty days. What measures can a foreman take during the probationary period to make certain that only competent workers are kept beyond the deadline?

Feedback—Are You Getting It?

An employment agency to which a worker who has quit goes to find another job may be getting stories you should be hearing. Here are two examples from one such agency's files—examples of feedback which was never fed back:

Employee #1: I feel I must make a change. I have given the job a chance for three years, and not one claim made by the recruiter has proved out. I am conscientious and a perfectionist in my work, but that has only made me enemies. Most people in the department are careless about their work, and they feel I make them look bad. They call me an "eager beaver."

Employee #2: They never made use of what I know, and before I get rusty I want to work for a company that does not discourage my initiative and that offers a chance for wider responsibility. Do you know what I've been doing for the past two years? I've been doing weekly updating of the change-journal part of an information-retrieval program. That's all I ever worked on. My boss told me I did the job better than anybody else ever had, and he wouldn't consider transferring me to another project.

A parting thought on discharge

"The only things that really end when a person is fired," an executive told a management gathering, "are his work and his wage. He (she) goes on—and a definite relationship between him and the company persists, even though he has been sawed off the payroll.

"In the first place, for a long time to come, he'll collar everyone he can get hold of, to chew the story of the events leading to his dismissal over and over again. That story will, naturally, be told from his point of view, and if the person is 'sore' the company is pretty sure to be pictured as a cold and soulless corporation. And Mrs. Ex-employee as well as the kids will be walking advertisements about the raw deal the old man got.

"All of which means that I worry more about the people I've fired than I do about those on the payroll. I want people to be fired in such a way that the company won't be hurt more than is absolutely necessary by their remarks while they're 'at liberty.'"

The Customer's-Eye View

Customer Satisfaction Isn't Everything

The president of a national corporation was impressed by the performance of a new dealership that had been opened the year before
in a territory that had hitherto been considered only marginal. No
one had been able to make much of a go of it before, and when, in
the most recent change, the Sales vice president had given it to Joe
Driver, everyone kept his fingers crossed.

But the last twelve months' record was astounding. The president decided to make Joe's operation the first port of call in his
swing around the territories. He buzzed his secretary and had her
arrange his itinerary accordingly.

The first thing the president noticed when he got to Joe's place
of business was a large sign in the showroom, and he later found it
repeated in small placards in the sales and accounting offices, and
prominently in the service department. The signs all read:

> **Customer Satisfaction Isn't Everything —
> IT's the ONLY Thing!**

The president liked the swing of that; it proclaimed a singleness
of purpose and a winning attitude. He made a note to have Cy
Harder, the Sales v.p., use it as the company's "slogan of the year"
with which they kicked off each year's national sales contest.

Signs, of course, don't work marvels by themselves, and slogans
alone don't turn an unprofitable territory into a profitable one. But

275

the digging the president was able to do into Joe's operations during his stay there and his checks with key customers in the territory produced ample evidence that Joe Driver backed up the slogan with solid performance. It was plain that Joe had hammered home to every man and woman in his organization that the dealership could thrive and grow only as a result of *repeat business*. And that meant only one thing—*satisfied customers*.

The evidence of Joe's philosophy was all around. It added up to what the president knew were "the three S's of success":

- *Sales:* The salesmen knew their stuff. They were well trained. They knew the company's products, and the special needs of their customers, and made full use of the company's product and service literature. They were more than order-takers; they followed through on application problems and on inventory planning, and knocked themselves out to take care of emergencies. They operated on a system of planned calls and analyses, and traded information in weekly sales meetings.
- *Service:* The service department was neat and shipshape, and the personnel were knowledgeable and courteous. Records were in tiptop shape, and were used for more than billing and accounting purposes. Customer "service profiles" were developed, and there was an effective system of customer reminders and follow-ups.
- *Support:* Finally, Joe knew the importance of "the man behind the man behind the gun" (and that went for women, too). The order clerks and the bookkeepers and the parts department personnel all knew that they were working for the customer.

The president made another note before he left Joe's operations—here was a man to keep an eye on. There was a lot more than the current dealership in his future!

How Not to Sell
a Vacuum Cleaner

Joe Curious and his wife, Eager, stopped in at a local discount house to look at the new Wondermatic vacuum cleaner that the manufacturer had been advertising in all of the women's magazines and on TV and in full-page newspaper ads.

"It powers itself, so you don't have to push it, just like your new power mower," Eager had enthused. "No other machine does that. And it goes backwards and forwards, and automatically adjusts to any carpet nap. Friendly & Cash have had a demonstrator model on display all week."

"Sounds like a good deal," Joe had replied. "You've been wanting a new vac for a long time." (After all, he had talked her into that new mower.) "Let's take a look." So here they were.

The demonstration model was right near the front door. The nearest salesman was busy with a customer looking at TVs, but Joe and Eager decided to try it out themselves. "Something's wrong with this handle grip," said Joe. Sure enough, the plastic grip was cracked and loose.

"Gee," said Eager, "the machine looks pretty beat up. Will ours look like this in a few weeks? Friendly & Cash have only had this one on display for five days."

The salesman ambled up. "Sorry to have held you up, folks," he apologized. "But that other customer was yack yacking about TVs for a half-hour and (he muttered under his breath) didn't buy after all. But lemme show off the wonderful Wondermatic."

"The handle's cracked," Joe pointed out.

"And it sure looks beat up," added Eager.

"Well, you know how people treat demonstration models," said the salesman. "But try her on this strip of rug." And after fiddling with the cracked handle grip a bit, he got it moving. "Try it, madam. When you push forward, it propels *itself* forward. When you pull back, it powers itself backwards. Saves *your* back."

"How does it work?" asked Joe, kneeling down to examine the machine. "Does it have a bumper that clicks it into reverse when you hit a piece of furniture?"

"I don't really know that technical detail," said the salesman. "All I know is that when I pull back on the handle grip, the cleaner goes backwards."

Joe examined the handle grip. "Oh," he said, "the handle grip's *supposed* to be loose, even though this one *is* cracked. When you pull back on the grip, it moves and actuates a switch that throws the machine into reverse."

"Whadya know," said the salesman, "you're right!"

"How about that automatic adjustment to the nap of the rug?" asked Joe. "Is there a pin mechanism of some sort that probes the depth of the rug and triggers another switching mechanism to raise or lower the agitator brush and suction head?"

The salesman scratched his head. "I don't know just how that happens," he said. "But I know it's automatic."

Again Joe crouched down and examined the underside of the machine. "Oh," he said, "here's the secret. These grooved rubber wheels float on top of the nap. When they raise or lower, the agitator brush and suction heads go up or down."

"Sure enough," agreed the salesman. "Now," he added briskly, "do you good folks have any other questions?" He whipped out his order book. "We still have a few of these Wondermatics in stock, but let me tell you, they're moving fast and the Wondermatic people can't promise us another delivery until—"

"Well, we'll just think it over and maybe be back later," said Joe and Eager, in chorus. And they left the store.

"By golly," said Joe, "that's an ingenious machine design. The way that reverse works is clever. But why the heck didn't Friendly & Cash fix that blamed handle grip? Maybe there are some other weak parts. But, Eager, isn't that floating drive clever? What do you think of their design?"

There was a long pause. Eager seemed deep in thought. "That machine looked pretty beat up to me," she said, finally.

Post-Mortem: Salesman Sam was certainly no whiz. He beefed about his previous customers, belittled customers who handled demonstration models, and couldn't answer the most elementary questions about his product. He didn't even keep his machine in tiptop working order and appearance. *But what about store management and Sam's supervisor?* (They were busy, probably counting overstocks!)

SCENARIO 113

The Extra Step
(Two Brief Scenes)

Scene: A busy international airport.

A stewardess is perched on a waiting-room chair, peering intently at some papers a man seated next to her has spread out on the open briefcase he's holding on his lap. He was one of her passengers on the flight that has just come in. Later she is seen accompanying him to the airport customs office.

It turns out (as the appreciative passenger later wrote to the president of the airline) that he had booked passage to accompany a shipment of 2,000 pounds of delicate instruments. The stewardess spent an entire morning of her very brief stopover time between flights to help him get them through customs, thereby enabling him to meet performance on a vital foreign contract.

Scene: Convention-exhibit area of a large New York hotel.

The three-day trade show is over, and workmen are dismantling the booths. The trade association executive who has been in charge of the successful convention and exhibit is watching them.

A hotel porter comes up to the executive and asks him please to step into a side room for a chat. The association executive is glad to comply; he knows the porter, for the man had been of great help in seeing to it that the exhibitors had everything they needed when they were setting up their displays.

As soon as they are alone, the porter proceeds to give the ex-

280

ecutive a most intensive sales talk on just why that trade association should return to that particular hotel the following year.

"If that porter's spark could be transmitted to the entire staff of the hotel," the executive says later, in recounting the experience, "the combination would be a working organization that no competition could equal!"

Sale Fail

A would-be customer had had a little windfall (an unexpected bonus) and decided to splurge on something he had wanted for a long time—one of those fairly expensive battery-powered watches that were supposed to be accurate within an umpteenth of a second for a long period. He went up to the jewelry counter in a large department store where a wide selection of watches was on display. One in particular caught his eye—a battery-powered watch with a manufacturer's name he recognized, and one that was not all that expensive, only a little over a hundred dollars.

The lady behind the counter kept him waiting a bit while she put away some stock and straightened up another part of the counter. Then she came over and asked whether she could help. The dialogue went something like this:

"I'm interested in this battery-powered watch. Can you tell me how accurate it is?"

"What do you mean, accurate? They're all very accurate."

"Well, what I want to know is how much might it gain or lose in, say a week or a month, or you name the period. I've seen some ads that say watches like this (of course, they may have been more expensive) keep time within a gnat's eyebrow for as much as a year."

"I wouldn't know about that, Sir. All I know is that they're supposed to be very accurate."

"But before I spend over a hundred dollars for a watch, I want to know how accurate I can expect it to be. By the way, how long have you been selling this new type of watch?"

282

"Almost a year now. Why?"

"Didn't anyone ever tell you, or weren't you ever curious to know, just how accurate a customer can expect them to be?"

"Well, all I know is that they're supposed to be very accurate."

No sale.

Customer Focus*

Scene: Quality Control office. The chief of Quality Control is discussing quality problems with the supervisor of the department where rejects have been running high on a telephone handset assembly job.

Quality Control Chief: Almost all of these rejects are due to carelessness in putting on this tiny bit of insulation on a soldered connection. Can't you do something about this, Frank?

Frank: I've tried about everything I know—instructing our people to be more careful, and so on. But my keeping at them about quality just doesn't seem to work.

Q. C. Chief: You'll have to think of something, Frank.

Follow-up reel: Frank is seen talking to a group of the assembly workers. He's hit upon the idea of giving them the full story of the *why* behind the job:

Frank (winding up): . . . and so you see, that's what happens to a telephone conversation when this innocent-looking piece of insulation is not properly placed. Nothing but meaningless noise.

Workers: Well, why didn't you tell us that *before?* We didn't know it made all that difference. Those guys over in Quality Control are always so fussy. We thought their yapping about the placement of that insulation was just somebody's fancy idea!

---

*Based on an experience recounted by J. Walter Dietz of Western Electric Company.

Trying on the Other Fellow's Shoes

Here's an idea some companies are following to get across the customer's-eye view: periodically, in some cases once a week, an employee (maybe someone right off the production floor) makes a full day of sales calls with a saleman. The factory worker hears praise and criticism and problems first hand, and gains fresh insight into how his individual efforts contribute.

"I didn't know what a salesman has to go through," said one veteran employee. "He has to take it from everybody!"

The Service Man and the Million-Dollar Advertising Budget

Mr. and Mrs. Cash had just bought an Apex-Acme color television set, console, twenty-one-inch screen. They had paid over $700 for it, and it was complete with all conceivable features: beautiful living color, magic push-bqtton tuning, instant voice and pictures, remote channel selection, ultrahigh frequency—in short, "the works."

The only trouble was that after installation, it didn't work properly. Pictures were fuzzy, people were purple, and they could get only one UHF channel, marred by a lot of snow.

But they weren't disturbed. The salesman had said this happened in some locations, and a call to Service would bring a man out promptly to make all necessary adjustments. They called, and the man came with satisfactory promptness. Mr. and Mrs. Cash hovered over him as he did his tinkering.

The serviceman's opening remarks were, "Well, I'll get this working for now. But I've got to warn you that this model, with all of its gadgets, is giving us a lot of trouble."

While he was bringing the purple people back to healthy color, he observed, "Wow! I can see that somebody's been playing around with these vertical/horizontal, brightness, and tint-control adjustments! You got any kids around here that you turned loose on this instrument?"

"Only one fifty-two-year-old boy," said Mrs. Cash. Mr. Cash didn't say anything.

The serviceman did some more adjusting, and then turned to Mr. Cash. "Look," he said, "I've got this working okay now. But what I don't understand is how you got it so out of kilter. Lemme see just what you do when you operate it."

The fifty-two-year-old boy stepped over and pressed the "on" button and the rainbow-tinted button next to it.

"Hey!" shouted the service man. "Not *that* button! Didn't you read the instructions? That's the manual-tuning activator that takes you off our factory service setting. Stay with the automatic." Mr. Cash followed instructions, and the picture came in bright and clear and correctly hued. The serviceman lit a cigarette, and looked at Mr. Cash reflectively. "Stay with the automatic," he said again, and paused. "I wouldn't advise you to try any finetuning on your own."

"Sorry, I thought I understood the instructions," said Mr. Cash. "But what about UHF?" He turned the appropriate dials, and succeeded in getting three stations with a better picture, but still pretty snowy. "How come we can't get any of those other stations?" he asked.

The serviceman looked at Mr. Cash witheringly. "You must be kidding, he said. "Did you expect to get good UHF in this area? How did you expect the unidirectional wave pattern to counteract the frequency modulating multiplexor effect of these high-rise condominiums?" (At least that's the way his technical explanation came across to Mr. Cash.) "I'm sure our sales department tried to explain that to you."

"Sorry again," replied Mr. Cash. "I should have known. But you can be sure I'll be in touch with the sales department about your excellent service. Don't forget your tools. And don't worry about those ashes on the carpet. Mrs. Cash will sweep them up."

"Okay," said the serviceman, gathering up his belongings. "Glad I fixed you up. No charge for *this* call, but with that model, I'll probably be seeing you soon. Goodbye for now."

Apex-Acme had a marvelous advertising agency. Its current theme: "Our customers are our closest friends," for which the budget was $1,000,000 per year.

Apex-Acme also had a good technical training organization. The servicemen it turned out knew their sets from A to Z, and it boasted that "they can fix 'em in the dark."

Too bad the two didn't get together!

"I Don't Get Enough Complaints"

NOTE: Could you and your department and other fellow employees live up to the following invitation, if the head of your company gave it? Here is a letter which the president of The Equitable Life Assurance Society of the United States addressed to all of the company's many thousand of policy holders:

I don't get enough complaints.
I mean it. I get a few, but I don't get enough. And I know we can't be doing everything that well.

Nothing is more vital to The Equitable's success than coming right with our policy owners. No measure of our performance can be as important as customer satisfaction.

We rely on the personal attention of a corps of Equitable Agents. They serve as representatives of the total Equitable, available to you life-long and nationwide. They are committed to serve. But sometimes things can go wrong over which our Agent has no control.

If you experience such difficulty with our service, I am asking you to let us know. You can use our toll-free 800 "Hot Line" from any point in the United States. Or you can write to me directly—personally—if you prefer. I'd like to hear from you.

We want you to feel very good about The Equitable. Customer satisfaction is worth a lot to us. Do us the favor of registering your dissatisfaction. Give us a chance to solve the problem.

We intend to fill your expectations 100 percent, 100 percent of the time. Please complain if we don't.
Signed: Roy Eklund
President

A parting thought about customers

If I were to come to work and find on my desk two pieces of paper, one a customer complaint, the other telling me our P&L was in a mess, I'd handle the complaint first.

—*Harry Mullikin*

PART FIVE

GET-AHEADS

Who's Your Competition?

NOTE: The following story was told at a presentation made by the president and other executives of the Rodney Hunt Machine Company at an American Management Associations symposium.

A young man began his working career with a company that had eleven hundred employees. Understandably, he felt rather discouraged about ever reaching a high position in this company because he was among the very lowest on the totem pole. After he had been working there a while, however, he saw a notice on the bulletin board saying that a prize of twenty-five dollars was being offered for workable suggestions, and he started sending in his ideas. After he had sent in six suggestions, one of them won a prize.

But it wasn't the prize that made the big impression on him and gave him the first "whiff of success" that ultimately led him to a top-level job. What fired his determination was the discovery he made, upon casual inquiry after receiving the award, that only twenty other employees had sent in suggestions.

He suddenly realized that in that company he was competing with only twenty people and not with eleven hundred!

The Case of the Unconfident Office Supervisor

Joe B——, age forty, was an excellent assistant supervisor in a large office department where he had worked since his graduation from high school. He supervised the preparation of numerous forms and other paperwork procedures, putting the finished documents on the supervisor's desk for signature.

Joe obviously liked his job, and was good at it. One day there was a sudden shift in his boss's responsibilities, and Joe was promoted to take his place as supervisor of the department. But then it developed that despite his ability to do the work, the responsibility of signing the papers seemed to be too much for him. He became sleepless, lost his appetite, began to put off making decisions, and in general dreaded each new day.

Fortunately, Joe realized that he had a serious problem, and went to his company's medical department for help. And again, luckily for Joe, the company was forward looking in its approach to problems of emotional distress in employees, and included professional counseling among its services. The counselor acquainted himself with the surrounding conditions, conferred with Joe's superiors, and had some long, sympathetic talks with Joe.

It soon developed that Joe's basic problem was a neurosis he had developed about his job. The other executives on his new level were all college graduates, and for that reason he had convinced himself that he would never make the grade. Overwhelmed by the fear of making a mistake, he developed an elaborate system of

294

keeping track of every little detail in his department. The result was an unmanageable flood of reports, checklists, and messages that descended on his desk every day.

In this case, Joe was once more fortunate, in that the vice president to whom he reported was an understanding individual. Alerted by the counselor, the vice president quietly began giving some extra encouragement to Joe. He frequently asked him to come in and discuss departmental matters, and offered occasional suggestions and reassurance.

Soon Joe became relaxed. He realized that his problem was one of his own creation—a "thing" about college graduates. To overcome an unjustified sense of inferiority, he had loaded himself with unnecessary backstopping in order to be one hundred percent informed on all details—something which nobody had ever expected him to be. He began delegating routines, and concentrated on his real job—managing.

Old-Job/New-Job Tangle

Did you ever back your car out of your garage, only to find that you're dragging along with it your garden hose and a rake and Junior's wagon—all of which somehow got tangled up with the front bumper? Maybe that's an exaggerated picture, and maybe it never actually happened to you. But it makes a point about managers that is worth underscoring.

It often happens that when a manager who has done an outstanding job in running his department is promoted to a bigger job, he is like the man we have just described. Figuratively speaking, he pulls along with him all kinds of entanglements with the job he has just left. His old department is just one of a number that now report to him, but instead of merely giving overall guidance and leadership to all of them, and devoting most of is time and energy to problems of coordination and long-range planning, he keeps concerning himself with the details of the operation he knows best—his old department—detracting from the efficiency and contributing to the frustration of the new man in charge.

The problem is by no means confined to middle-management jobs. A management cusultant tells of the chairman of a huge public transit authority. He had been elevated from the position of general superintendent, where, as a hardhitting operating executive who had spent all of his business life in mass transportation, he had made an outstanding record. But the trouble was, says the consultant, that he "took his old job upstairs with him"—including three telephones on his desk through which he could bark orders to all down the line. Many a top-level meeting was interupted by the

296

new general superintendent who had come in with his aids and unrolled blueprints on the conference-room table to get his boss's okay.

The chairman lived his job around the clock and made colorful copy for the media by taking personal charge of jamups and mishaps in operations. But the long-range program of the authority suffered. What was actually a double job of chairman and general superintendent left too little time for reflections on policy decisions, for the fundamentals of statesmanlike labor relations and future service plans for the sprawling city.

Moral: When that welcome promotion comes, don't carry excess clutter with you from the old job. Be careful how you back out of the garage!

Completed Staff Work

There were two supervisors, Harry and Larry. Each had what he thought was a terrific idea for solving a long-standing problem about bottlenecks in his department, and each idea called for spending roughly the same amount of money on some equipment and rearranging.

Both talked to the plant manager about their ideas. The manager said the same thing to each one: "Sounds good. Gimme a memo and maybe a little sketch, so I have something to take upstairs with me to get the necessary authorization."

Harry and Larry each complied with the request. A few days later, the boss told Harry that the idea was approved, and work would begin one it that very week. But he told Larry that there were "a lotta questions about that proposal, a lotta questions." He asked for more details, and Larry gave them to him the next day. But nothing happened, and Larry fumed and sweated, and his nose was out of joint when he saw the rearrangements going on in Harry's department.

Both ideas were good. What happened?

The secret of Harry's success was that he had heard about the concept of "Completed Staff Work," and practiced it. This is a concept and phrase popularized some years ago in the military. Here is how Major General Archer L. Learch has defined it (just substitute "supervisor" for "staff officer" and "management" for "head of staff division" in the following, and you'll see why Harry's idea had such smooth sailing):

Completed Staff Work as defined by the Army is the study of a problem, and the presentation of a solution, by a staff officer in such form that all remains to be done on the part of the head of the staff division, or the commander, is to indicate the approval or disapproval of the completed action

The words "completed action" are emphasized because the more difficult the problem, the greater the tendency to present it to the chief in piecemeal fashion. It is your duty as staff officer to work out the details. You should not consult your chief in the determination of those details. You may and should consult other staff officers and take advantage of all available specialized assistance. The end result should, when presented to the chief for approval or disapproval, be worked out in finished form.

The impulse which often comes to the inexperienced staff officer, to ask the chief what to do, recurs more often when the problem is difficult. It's so easy to ask the chief what to do, and it appears easy for him to answer. Resist that impulse!

The theory of completed staff work does not preclude a rough draft, but the rough draft must not be a *half-baked* one. It must be complete in every respect except that it lacks the requisite number of copies and need not be in final neat form. But rough draft must not be used as an excuse for shifting to the chief the burden of formulating the action.

The final test is this: if you were the chief, would you be willing to sign the paper you have prepared, and stake your professional reputation on its being right.

If the answer is in the negative, take it back and work it over, because it is not yet *completed* staff work.

The Boss's-Eye View

Nate Ollings had submitted a suggestion to the factory manager about the desirability of a new piece of equipment for the cartoning department. To him it was an open-and-shut case. True, there would be an initial investment of over $18,000 for the machine, some conveyor equipment, and the necessary controls. But with increased output and the saving of the equivalent of one and a half women on the line, the equipment would easily pay for itself in three years at the most.

The idea was reviewed, and a couple of weeks later the manager told Nate it had been turned down. "It was good thinking, though, Nate," the boss had said. "I'm tied up today and tomorrow, but I'll give you the whys and wherefores after the bowling match Friday night."

Nate was teed off. "What was there to discuss? What was the matter with those stupid jerks in the front office? What was the matter with the boss, anyway? Were you supposed to twist his arm to see a good thing? Where else could the company get a return on its money like that?" The more he thought about it, the more burned up he became. He sounded off in no uncertain terms about the front office and the boss at lunch, in discussing it with the man in charge of the cartoning line. Ted had helped him with some of the details of the proposal.

On Friday night, as promised, Nate's boss had a quiet, uninterupted discussion with him about the cartoning operation, over a couple of beers after the bowling game. Here Nate got a slant at the "boss's-eye view"—at the kind of considerations management has to think about with regard to an "open-and-shut" proposition.

The boss gave him some facts of life about financial ratios on the company's balance sheet. This wasn't a big company, and management had to be pretty careful about $18,000.

First, there was such a thing as "current ratio"—simply stated, the amount of money available to meet upcoming outgo, like taxes, supplies, and payroll. Then, the banks and others interested in the company's credit rating took a dim view of having too much money tied up in "fixed assets"—bricks and mortar and machines. And there had to be enough working capital to finance the company's expected sales volume. And anyway, with some product changes in the offing, that whole cartoning setup might have to be completely restructured in less than two years. And more.

" . . . and so you see, Nate," the boss wound up, "the simple fact of the matter is that there are a lot of other places where that $18,000 will come in handy. *The job of management is one continued balancing act.*"

It all made Nate think a little better about the "jerks in the front office." (He wished now that he hadn't sounded off quite so strongly at lunch the other day. He'd make a point, tomorrow, to talk again to Ted, over at the cartoning line.)

Al Fielding's Big Mistake

Supervisor Al Fielding asked for an opportunity to talk to the plant manager in private. The manager immediately made room for him in his schedule, and saw to it that his secretary would not be present during the meeting.

Al had a grievance and wanted to get it off his chest. "Why wasn't I given that promotion as your assistant when your right-hand man was promoted to head up at the Blankville plant?" he wanted to know. "Bill got the job when he hadn't been here nearly as long as I have. I've got ten years' experience to his five!"

The plant manager took time out to go rather thoroughly into the requirements for the "assistant-to" job in question. And in the course of the discussion he took occasion to remind the disgruntled supervisor that he hadn't seen fit to enroll in any of the numerous after-hours executive-development programs the company had offered over the years, including some tuition-paid evening courses at the local college. "And Bill grabbed at everything of that sort that came his way," he added.

"But I've got the *experience*," Al protested. "Ten years of it. I know my job inside out, and I haven't pulled any boners like some of those hair-brained 'improvements' Bill tried out in his department."

"Maybe that's where you made your biggest mistake, Al," said the manager, interrupting him. "Sure, I've let Bill try out a lot of his ideas, even though on occasion I suspected that what he wanted to do might not work out. And Bill's got some rough edges, I'll admit. But I'd rather slow down a fast horse than try to speed up a slow one." And then he concluded the discussion with a gentle clincher: "You haven't had ten years' experience, Al," he said softly, "you've had one year's experience ten times in a row."

Your "Profile" for the Job Ahead

The evening meal was over, the dishes had been cleared away, and Frank Cutler's oldest daughter was already aproned and sloshing soapy water in the dishpan. Frank had had an especially rough day as Machine Room supervisor at the plant, and his wife had fully expected him to draw up the easy chair in front of the television set and settle down for his favorite Sports-Review-of-the-Week program.

Instead, he had poured himself another cup of coffee and taken it to the desk in the corner of the living room. He had shoved aside the papers on which his wife had been doing some battling with household budgets and upcoming bills, and was busy at work on some papers of his own.

"What are you doing, dear," Mrs. Culter called to him, "writing the first chapter of your autobiography?" And she came up to him and peered over his shoulder.

"No," said Frank, "nothing that grand." But then he paused, reflected a little, and added, "but maybe I am at that, in a way. Maybe this is really the beginning of a new chapter." He showed her a chart he'd been working on and explained what he was doing.

Frank had a good job as supervisor, but he had his eyes on bigger things at the plant. He didn't intend to remain supervisor. He had a great deal of admiration and respect for his immediate superior, Jim Hathaway, the assistant plant manager. Jim was a

304

good man, and was bound to be made plant manager in the next couple of years, since pretty good rumor had it that the old man was going to move out and up to vice president at corporate headquarters.

Frank saw no reason why he shouldn't be bucking for Jim's job. But he'd come across a proverb on the flyleaf of his younger daughter's English reader, and it had started him thinking. The proverb was, "If wishes were horses, beggers might ride."

Frank knew he wasn't ready as yet for Jim's job. Clearly something more than wishing was called for. What he had been working on, and was now explaining to his wife, was an analysis he had made of the job ahead—Jim's job—and how at the moment he, Frank Cutler, stacked up against the requirements.

Down the left-hand side of the sheet of paper he was now pointing at, Frank had listed all the major components he could think of that combined to make up Jim's job. He also included some important "man specifications" as he saw them, that Jim embodied to hold his own in the job. It was no small list. Here are some representative job factors, as a sample:

- *Production Scheduling and Equipment Loading.* Frank had similar responsibilities within his department, regarding detailed assignments and loading to meet weekly and monthly quotas; but Jim drew up the figures plantwide, and much farther into the future, for discussion and authorization at the weekly manager's meetings.
- *Quality Control.* Frank had boned up on the techniques and charts of the Statistic Quality Control boys and was pretty hep to the use of the charts and control points to forestall quality problems. Jim was more so, as regarded *all* departments.
- *Inventory Control.* Frank had little to do with this, beyond his own work-in-process; Jim had final decisions here, using relevant staff-prepared graphs and control limits.
- *Dealing with the Union.* Frank had participated—and had been sustained—in a few arbitration hearings and in general was on good terms with the shop steward. But union matters were a pretty big and frequent part of Jim's job.

And there were a number of other important job factors. As to "man specifications," here are some of the things Frank had jotted down:

- *Education*
- *Job Experience*
- *Personality*
- *"Friction Record"*

And a number of others.

Frank's next move was to analyze himself as honestly as he could against the factors he had listed, to see how he stacked up as a "substitute Jim." He knew that he obviously wouldn't bat 1,000, so he allowed room for jotting down some indicated action, or notation *re* current action. Here is how his analysis looked:

To the right of the list, he had five columns, headed by the numbers 1,2,3,4, and 5. The remaining broad column to the right was headed "Remarks," for the notations mentioned above. Following, this is the legend defining the numbers heading up the columns, as they referred to the job factors. (For the man specifications, they simply indicated gradations ranging from "poor" to "excellent"):

1. No knowledge or experience.
2. Well-informed "layman's knowledge," little or no direct experience.
3. Knowledge as above, or somewhat more, with some direct experience.
4. Knowledge as above, or better, with considerable direct experience (several years).
5. Exceptional knowledge, including theoretical base backed up by several years experience.

With the above as a framework, Frank put a heavy black "bullet" in the appropriate column for each factor. Where the bullets were in columns lower than no. 4, he had something in the "Remarks" column.

No need to go into Frank's particular "profile" any further here. The big question is, how would *yours* look for "the job ahead"?

Which Supervisor Got the Promotion?

The vice president for Manufacturing was in from the home office, and had been discussing matters in general with the plant manager. "By the way," he said, "how about that promotion you're going to make? You've got two pretty good men in Art Goodman and Jim Brighter. I guess it's pretty tough to make a choice, eh?"

"Oh, not so tough," answered the plant manager. "I think I can demonstrate." He picked up the phone and asked the girl outside to page Art Goodman and have him come in. "Art and Jim were both involved in that fru-fru we had with the Goldfinch job," he remarked to the v.p. "I guess you remember that one."

"Don't I ever," said the v.p. "I thought sure we'd lose them for good!"

In a few minutes, Art Goodman came in.

"Art, " said the plant manager, "We've been discussing the Goldfinch account. How do we stand on that now, you remember that mixup we had."

"I'll let you know in a minute," said Art, and hurried out. In just about a minute he was back. "We're right on the ball with their current order," he reported. "Those 2,000 widgets scheduled for shipment on Friday will go out on time."

"How did we finally come out on those nonmatching frobush flanges they were screaming about?" asked the plant manager.

"I'll get you that dope, too," said Art, and popped out again. In five minutes (more or less), he was back. "Those frobush flanges came back last Monday," he reported. "We put in overtime on reworking them and the okay sets went out this morning. That was a half-day later than promised, but when Jim Brighter checked with me on that yesterday, he said he'd call Goldfinch's purchasing manager."

"Any backlash from Goldfinch?" the plant manager wanted to know.

"Well," said Art, "I haven't heard of any."

"Okay," replied the plant manager. "We won't hold you up anymore. Ask Marge to page Jim Brighter and have him come in."

When Jim Brighter came in, the plant manager repeated the scenario exactly. "Jim," he said, "we've been discussing the Goldfinch account. How do we stand on that now? You remember that mixup we had."

"Boy, do I remember it!" said Jim. "Art and I have been riding herd on that one. Their 2,000 widgets scheduled for shipment on Friday will definitely go out on time. Those nonmatching frobush flanges that caused all the flap came back last Monday. We put in overtime on reworking them and the okay sets went out this morning. When Art told me we would miss the promise date on them by half a day, I went over to Goldfinch's personally, to see if that caused any problems, and whether there was anything we could do on upcoming shipments to help their schedules. I'm pretty sure the Goldfinch people are happy again."

"Fine," said the plant manager. "No need to keep you further, Jim."

After Jim left, the plant manager looked at the v.p. and spread out his hands.

"I see what you mean," said the v.p.

From the Horse's Mouth

Harry Restive had for some time been thinking about changing jobs. He had told a few friends outside, and had received an invitation for an interview held the previous Saturday, from XYZ Company. This had developed into a firm offer, and Harry had to come to a decision.

This was obviously going to be an important decision, and Harry had sought out a friend of his father's, Mr. Vetran, for some advice. Mr. Vetran had a responsible job as head of one of the other departments in the company where Harry was a supervisor. He was a sort of sponsor of Harry; in fact, he'd gotten Harry his job there some years ago, and had given him valuable pointers over the years. Let's tune in one their conversation:

Mr. Vetran: So you really want to leave ABC? What's the big problem—ABC's a fine company, and I hear you're well thought of.

Harry: There's nothing wrong with ABC. Its just that I want to get ahead, not only in money, but in opportunity. Frank Gohard [Harry's immediate boss, and assistant plant manager] is a swell guy to work for, even if a bit of a driver. Mr. Tuffer [the plant manager] runs a good operation. But where do I go from here? Frank's about my age, and I'm not sure he'd move up to the top job in the plant if that were to open. Mr. Tuffer will probably be around a long time, and there are at least three "crown princes."

Mr. Vetran: I can't blame you for being ambitious, and XYZ is a good outfit. But I've seen young fellows make some serious mistakes in situations like this. I won't presume to advise—the decision is yours. But I can offer you a five-point "prescription," if you want it, based on my own experience and observations. If I could put it in a bottle, maybe it should be labeled "Shade well and take before making a job-switch decision."

Harry: I"ll buy the "bottle." That's why I came to see you.

Mr. Vetran: Okay—here goes:

First, take a good look at your present job. Have you looked at *all* the angles and opportunities? I've seen fellows leave a job because they claimed it didn't measure up to their qualifications and ambitions, and couldn't lead anywhere, only to have a live-wire successor come in on the same job and make it expand and grow. Often the first fellow would overlook the fact that the company's expanding operations would be bound to increase the job opportunities. He judged his job as a static thing when the whole surrounding situation was dynamic.

Second, don't go in over your head. An ambitious, well-spoken young fellow may oversell himself to another employer by putting a very, very, best foot forward in talking about past experience and his present job. And the lure of a big jump in salary may make him take on a job for which he is not well enough seasoned or well enough trained. This can cause a lot of headaches and frustrations, and unless he manages to pull himself up by his bootstraps, he may end up by losing out on the new job, with a black mark on his record and some sears on his self-confidence.

Third, know something about the internal "people problems" you're running into. Were some of the key people whom you'll be working with, or who may even report to you, gunning for the job? Are they going to lead to difficulties? (That's no reason for *not taking* a job, but it pays to go into a situation like that with your eyes open!)

Fourth, what about your new boss? Can you find out something about experiences others have had in working for him? *Does he know his stuff?* Will he help you grow? Or will he hold you down? I've known cases where the main reason a fellow changed jobs was that he couldn't get along with his boss—only to find that the new boss was as even worse so-and-so! (Of course, there's always the chance that the real problem was inside themselves, and not with the boss.)

Fifth, finally, if you *do* make a change, be sure you do everything possible to leave under the best possible circumstances. Give the longest possible notice. Leave everything shipshape. And never, *never* "sound off"—no matter what grievances you may have had, or think you have had. Remember, you may want to come back some day, or want a reference! You never can tell.

Well, that's the prescription, with five ingredients. Mix well and take before deciding.

Harry: Thanks, "Doc" Vetran. I'll take as prescribed.

A parting thought on getting ahead

"Well, in *our* country," said Alice, still panting a little, "you'd generally get to somewhere else—if you ran very fast for a long time, as we've been doing."

"A slow sort of country!" said the Queen. "Now, *here*, you see, it takes all the running you can do, to keep in the same place. It you want to get somewhere else, you must run at least twice as fast."

—Lewis E. Carroll,
Through the Looking Glass

INDEX

Index

5

9-81
3